First Steps in SAP® Business Warehouse (BW)

Gerardo di Giuseppe

Gerardo di Giuseppe
First Steps in SAP® Business Warehouse (BW)

ISBN:	978-1-5120-0758-9
Editor:	Alice Adams
Proofreading:	Tracey Duffy
Cover Design:	Philip Esch, Martin Munzel
Cover Photo:	Fotolia #52026918 (c) magann
Interior Design:	Johann-Christian Hanke

All rights reserved.

1st Edition 2015, Gleichen

© 2015 by Espresso Tutorials GmbH

URL: www.espresso-tutorials.com

All rights reserved. Neither this publication nor any part of it may be copied or reproduced in any form or by any means or translated into another language without the prior consent of Espresso Tutorials GmbH, Zum Gelenberg 11, 37130 Gleichen, Germany.

Espresso Tutorials makes no warranties or representations with respects to the content hereof and specifically disclaims any implied warranties of merchantability or fitness for any particular purpose. Espresso Tutorials assumes no responsibility for any errors that may appear in this publication.

Feedback
We greatly appreciate any kind of feedback you have concerning this book. Please mail us at *info@espresso-tutorials.com*.

Table of Contents

Preface		**5**
1	**Introduction to SAP BW 7.3**	**7**
1.1	Business intelligence and SAP BW	7
1.2	First steps with SAP BW 7.3	12
1.3	Summary	17
2	**Basic objects in the SAP BW layer**	**19**
2.1	InfoProviders	19
2.2	InfoObjects in brief	20
2.3	InfoCubes in brief	21
2.4	DataStore Object (DSO) in brief	23
2.5	MultiProviders in brief	25
2.6	InfoSets in brief	25
2.7	VirtualProviders in brief	28
2.8	The Data Warehousing Workbench (DWW)	28
2.9	InfoObjects in detail	30
2.10	InfoCubes in detail	41
2.11	Summary	46
3	**The SAP ETL process**	**47**
3.1	Extraction	47
3.2	Transformation	58
3.3	Loading	62
3.4	Recap of the ETL process	67
3.5	Summary	68
4	**Administration tools and process chains**	**69**
4.1	The administration functions	69

	4.2	Managing InfoCubes	72
	4.3	Managing a DataStore (DSO)	77
	4.4	Process chains	82
	4.5	Summary	88
5	**SAP BI Content**		**89**
	5.1	The purpose of BI Content	89
	5.2	Overview of BI Content objects	89
	5.3	Versions of the BI Content objects	91
	5.4	Activating BI Content objects	92
	5.5	Metadata Repository	98
	5.6	Summary	100
6	**Data access optimizations**		**101**
	6.1	About BW system performance	101
	6.2	Using aggregates	101
	6.3	BW statistics	108
	6.4	Summary	111
7	**Designing queries**		**113**
	7.1	Business Explorer (BEx) tools	113
	7.2	BEx Query Designer overview	114
	7.3	Creating a query	118
	7.4	Summary	136
8	**Reporting**		**137**
	8.1	SAP reporting tools	137
	8.2	BEx Analyzer	137
	8.3	Summary	147
A	**About the Author**		**149**
B	**Index**		**150**
D	**Disclaimer**		**153**

Preface

It has been said that in his life, a man should plant a tree, start a family, and write a book. I made all of those things happen for me in 2014 (what a year)! Even though writing a book was not on my radar, getting in touch with Martin Munzel and Alice Adams at Espresso Tutorials convinced me that I could share my passion for business intelligence with readers like you who want to evaluate and learn more about SAP Business Warehouse software.

During the last decade, the information technology world has been hit by lightning speed technological developments. This is leading to the accumulation of an immense amount of data, the likes of which has never seen before. Companies understand the value of using this new flow of information and IT departments are expected to put an infrastructure in place that will allow for the analysis of this new data. One essential piece of that infrastructure is the data warehouse (DWH), which has the primary purpose of pulling data out of source systems, adapting the data to company requirements, and returning the information to the business users in a way that they can understand and use it to make better business decisions. Hence the birth of business intelligence (BI).

In this book, my goal is to provide you with a first taste of one of the BI solutions in SAP Business Warehouse 7.3.

The book is structured in three main sections:

The first section familiarizes you with the most important BI and DWH terminology and provides an overview of SAP BW.

The second section provides a guide to the implementation and maintenance of a DWH with practical examples and useful tips.

Finally, the last section unveils how to make the data available to users by means of reports.

A few (well...many) months have now passed since I started this book-writing journey and I am happy to present you with the first mini-guide to SAP BW 7.3.

I dedicate this book to my beautiful, brilliant, and delightful wife who has tolerated me over the past several months and through the long hours spent writing this book.

We have added a few icons to highlight important information. These include:

Tips

Tips highlight information concerning more details about the subject being described and/or additional background information.

Warnings

Warnings draw attention to information that you should be aware of when you go through the examples from this book on your own.

Finally, a note concerning the copyright: All screenshots printed in this book are the copyright of SAP SE. All rights are reserved by SAP SE. Copyright pertains to all SAP images in this publication. For simplification, we will not mention this specifically underneath every screenshot.

1 Introduction to SAP BW 7.3

This chapter introduces you to business intelligence and SAP Business Warehouse. I will define common business intelligence terms and describe the first steps in SAP BW.

1.1 Business intelligence and SAP BW

With advances in technology and the resulting new business opportunities, the complexity of enterprise applications has dramatically increased over the last few decades. This has increased the volume of data that companies and their business partners and customers generate and has led to the necessity of even more sophisticated systems for operational, planning, and analytical applications. The enormous amount of electronic data can be seen as a huge benefit in terms of information that a company could retrieve to enhance its business performance, and this is ultimately the purpose of any analytical system or business intelligence platform. Since operative systems must be available at all times and must have response times in the seconds range for business transactions, they cannot be stressed with heavy workloads for running analytical calculations. This technological limitation has made it necessary to separate operative systems from analytical systems into two distinct enterprise applications, each with its own database and even different data layouts.

Business intelligence systems provide solutions for covering the entire process of retrieving the source data, transforming it into the data structures required, and providing the data structures for analysis. As a prerequisite, a specific database must be conceived in what is commonly called a *data warehouse (DWH)*. This design includes creating solid *metadata* (business and technical attributes and descriptions for the data objects). In addition, DWHs need to consolidate and create homogenous global master data, as well massive amounts of transaction data with differing degrees of aggregation.

1.1.1 What is an OLTP system?

Online Transaction Processing (OLTP) systems are operational systems dedicated to the company's business to assist in the daily management of tasks and they are therefore directly operational. The trend is to use an ERP (Enterprise Resource Planning) system, which includes all business activities (finance, human resources, logistics, sales, etc.) in a single configurable software organized around a database, thereby reducing communication costs between applications. OLTP systems typically comply with the ACID standard (see http://dev.mysql.com/doc/refman/5.6/en/mysql-acid.html). These criteria ensure that a database always has consistent and complete data, designed around a relational schema. The data stored represents the daily activities of a company at a high level of detail. ERP systems are primarily based on the OLTP concept.

1.1.2 What is an ERP system?

Enterprise Resource Planning systems are operational systems used to support the day-to-day activities of a company. ERP software facilitates the sharing of information among company departments such as human resources, purchasing, sales and distribution, manufacturing, financial accounting, and controlling. This sharing is accomplished thanks to a central database that all departments have access to (according to their access rights). ERP systems focus on integration, meaning that any data discontinuity or inconsistency is prevented. SAP was one of the first companies to introduce software that helps companies manage their daily work. SAP ERP is considered the most successful and complete ERP system available today.

1.1.3 What is an OLAP system?

Online Analytical Processing (OLAP)) systems provide key information to the management of a company. This information is needed to make appropriate business decisions based on the data available internally (ERP, CRM, databases) or externally (Internet, suppliers) to the company. The information system that can process this type of data is commonly called a data warehouse (e.g., SAP BW). Data required for decision processes is derived from various sources and aggregated. Thus, data is extracted, transformed, and loaded (*ETL process*) from an operational system such as SAP ERP to an analytical one (e.g., SAP BW)) for more complex analyses.

1.1.4 What is multidimensional modeling?

OLAP systems are designed to answer multi-dimensional database queries, in contrast to OLTP data models. Multi-dimensional data models are often visualized using a *data cube*. A typical question for this kind of schema might be: "Considering the sales activity, how many shoes (product) did we sell in March (period) in Venice (location)?" (see Figure 1.1). The axes of the analysis are called *dimensions* and there can be as many as the technology allows. Usually 13 dimensions are more than enough to describe a business activity (e.g., sales).

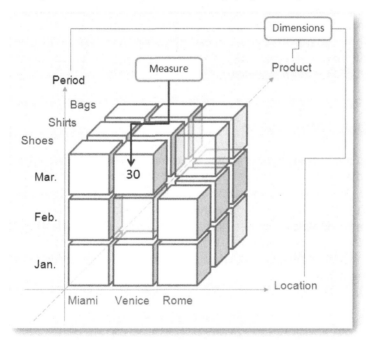

Figure 1.1: Multidimensional data cube

Dimensions (Characteristics)

Dimensions are the axes of the analysis and together they describe a *fact* (in Figure 1.1 it is a sale). Each cell in the data cube represents an occurrence of a fact. In SAP BW, dimensions are designed using *charac-*

teristics. They contain a set of values, e.g., the dimension *location* can take the value Miami, Venice, or Rome.

Measure (key figures)

The *measure* quantifies the fact to be analyzed and thus, is a value that has meaning for the analysis. In Figure 1.1, the sales fact is identified using the measure "quantity sold", e.g., 30 shoes were sold in Venice in March. In SAP BW, measures are called *key figures*.

Hierarchies

Dimensions can be grouped into different levels. For example, period can be grouped by quarter (January, February, and March) and location by country. This requires the creation of predefined hierarchies which are specified on the dimensions only. The lowest level of a dimension defines the granularity of the analysis, i.e., you cannot analyze the weekly sales if the lowest value of the dimension *period* is a month.

1.1.5 What is a star schema?

The *star schema* is the most commonly used multi-dimensional model for OLAP implementation. The data cube is stored as a star model as shown in Figure 1.2. The star has a fact table at its center, surrounded by several dimension tables. The fact table contains two kinds of attributes: the primary keys to dimension tables and the measures. Dimension tables correspond to the axes of the cube. Note that the number of dimensions and the number of measures are limited only by the technology used to implement the schema.

1.1.6 Main differences between OLTP and OLAP systems

Figure 1.3 highlights the main differences between OLTP and OLAP system design.

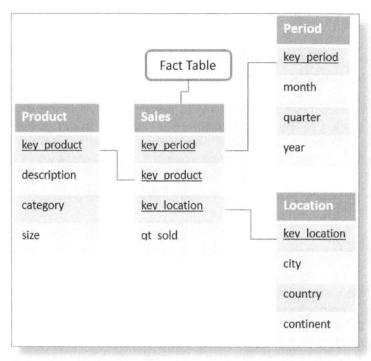

Figure 1.2: Example of a star schema

About	OLTP	OLAP
Data	Detailed, up-to-date	Summarized, historical
DB design	Highly normalized with many tables	De-normalized, few tables in a star schema
Query	Simple and standardized	Complex and ad-hoc
DB size	Mega-gigabytes	Giga-terabytes
Purpose	For fundamental business activities	For decision support and problem solving
Users	IT professionals	Decision makers

Figure 1.3: Main differences between OLTP and OLAP

1.2 First steps with SAP BW 7.3

SAP Business Warehouse is the business intelligence solution provided by SAP for reporting and data analysis. Data is extracted and loaded into SAP BW after being identified from the different systems. It is then transformed into multi-dimensional structures to prepare it for analyses. The OLAP tools in the SAP Business Explorer (BEx) suite are used to create reports. SAP BW comes pre-loaded with *business content*. It provides data structures, queries, and reports for multiple functional areas within a company (production, finance, etc.). SAP business content can receive data from all of the SAP systems (SAP CRM, ERP, SCM, etc.).

1.2.1 History

SAP BW version 1.2a was born in 1998 and had several pre-delivered *operational data stores (ODS)*, a star schema model called InfoCubes, and an Excel interface called Business Explorer (BEx). In version 2.0a, the ODS was renamed *persistent staging area (PSA)* and a new true ODS was introduced. The star schema model was simplified. Version 3.0a allowed data to be accessed from non-SAP sources and XML was supported. In 2004, BW entered maturity with the 3.5 release. It was now part of NetWeaver, Unicode was supported for the first time, and connectors Microsoft BI OLE and BI XMLA for web-based OLAP sources were added. The 2006 release added the BEx Query Designer, a graphical interface for ETL, and the Administrator Workbench was replaced with a new version called *Data Warehousing Workbench*. This book covers SAP BW 7.3, which started to move into in-memory database technology thanks to SAP HANA. The new version SAP BW 7.4 (released in March 2014) is the first version that takes full advantage of the new SAP HANA in-memory technology.

1.2.2 The BW data flow and architecture layers

SAP BW has three architecture layers:

1. The data acquisition layer
2. The data warehouse layer
3. The reporting layer

The data flows through these layers as shown in Figure 1.4.

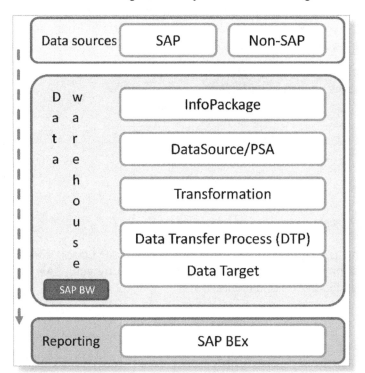

Figure 1.4: Data flows in SAP BW architecture

The data is collected from SAP and non-SAP source systems, such as Database Connect (DB), Universal Data Connect (UD), Web services, SAP Data Services (new as of BW 7.3), flat files, and from staging BAPIs (Business Application Programming Interfaces). Data is extracted in pull mode using InfoPackage objects. It is then temporarily stored in the staging area (PSA) before the transformations from the source format to the desired destination format take place. Afterwards, the loading process of adding transformed data to data targets using the *data transfer process (DTP)* begins. The reporting layer finally presents the data in reports and dashboards useful for decision-makers. The reporting components are housed in the SAP Business Explorer (BEx) suite.

1.2.3 Navigation in SAP BW

To use SAP BW, SAP GUI must first be installed on your PC. Then, with the user ID and password, you can log into the SAP BW system. The illustrations used in this book refer to SAP GUI installation for Windows. Follow the menu path START MENU • PROGRAMS • SAP FRONT END • SAP LOGON. Initially, you will see the SAP screen in Figure 1.5. Then, select the SAP system you want to log on to.

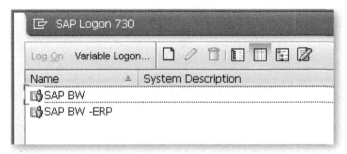

Figure 1.5: SAP initial screen

Clicking on the LOGON button will bring you to the SAP LOGON screen where you will have to enter the credentials provided by your SAP Administrator (see Figure 1.5 and Figure 1.6).

Figure 1.6: SAP logon screen

1.2.4 SAP Easy Access

Once you have successfully logged on, the SAP EASY ACCESS screen appears (see Figure 1.7).

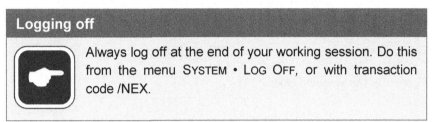

Logging off

Always log off at the end of your working session. Do this from the menu SYSTEM • LOG OFF, or with transaction code /NEX.

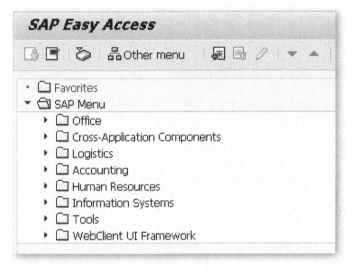

Figure 1.7: The SAP Easy Access screen

1.2.5 SAP Easy Access elements

Menu bar

The menu displayed depends on the application you are currently working on (see Figure 1.8). It may contain sub-menus.

Figure 1.8: The menu bar

15

Standard toolbar

The standard toolbar is available on every SAP screen (see Figure 1.9). Some icons may be deactivated depending on the application you are using. You can find out what each icon does when you run the cursor over it.

Figure 1.9: The standard toolbar

Application toolbar

The application toolbar contains the icons available in the current application (see Figure 1.10).

Figure 1.10: The application toolbar icons for SAP Easy Access

Command field

The command field is part of the menu bar and is hidden by default. Make it visible by pressing the arrow OPEN COMMAND FIELD and then enter the code to start a transaction Figure 1.11.

Figure 1.11: The command field

Transaction codes

Transaction codes are used as an alternative to a menu path. Every transaction in SAP BW is assigned to a code. For example, transaction code RSA1 starts the *Data Warehousing Workbench (DWW)*.

1.2.6 The SAP Easy Access menu

The SAP EASY ACCESS menu is the default entry point to the SAP system (see Figure 1.7). Navigation through the tree structure is based on your system rights. Double-clicking an entry will start the corresponding transaction. Frequently used transactions can be moved to the FAVORITES folder via drag-and-drop.

> **Multiple sessions**
>
> You can open up to six transactions in parallel. Precede the transaction code with either **/N** to open the transaction in the same window, or **/O** for a new window. The menu SYSTEM • CREATE SESSION will also open a new session.

1.3 Summary

In this chapter, I introduced you to the most important business intelligence terminology. I also provided a first glance at SAP BW software. Next, we'll look at the basic objects in the SAP BW layer.

2 Basic objects in the SAP BW layer

This chapter focuses on all types of InfoProviders available in SAP BW. We will then look at InfoObjects and InfoCubes (the star schema) in detail because they are the foundation of multidimensional modeling in SAP BW. You will learn how to create, administer, maintain, and monitor the data structure and data objects using the Data Warehousing Workbench (DWW).

2.1 InfoProviders

InfoProviders are objects that provide data for a query. They can be *persistent* (data is stored physically and persistently) or *non-persistent* (they provide only data stored in other objects such as data targets).

> **Queries and InfoProviders**
>
>
> A query can only be based on a single InfoProvider. The non-persistent InfoProviders are often used to combine data from various persistent InfoProviders and present the results as if they were one source.

2.1.1 The InfoProviders list

The persistent InfoProviders (also called *data targets*) are mainly the **InfoObject**, **DataStore Object (DSO)**, and the **InfoCube**. The non-persistent InfoProviders are the **MultiProvider**, **InfoSet**, and the **VirtualProvider** (see Figure 2.1). From SAP BW 7.3 on, new advanced InfoProviders are available to respond to new technologies (e.g., in-memory database), including: **BWA only InfoCube, semantically partitioned objects (SPO), Hybrid Provider, analytical index, Composite Provider,** and **TransientProvider**.

2.2 InfoObjects in brief

InfoObjects (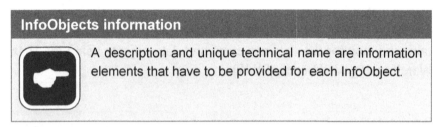) are the basic building blocks of SAP BW. They are the basis for defining or configuring all of the other InfoProviders. They can also act as InfoProviders themselves.

> **InfoObjects information**
>
> 👉 A description and unique technical name are information elements that have to be provided for each InfoObject.

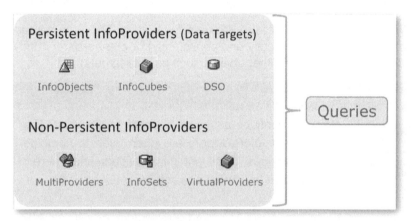

Figure 2.1: Basic SAP BW InfoProviders

2.2.1 Five types of InfoObjects

There are five types of InfoObjects: Deutschland

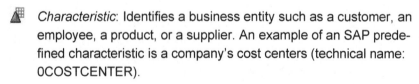

Characteristic: Identifies a business entity such as a customer, an employee, a product, or a supplier. An example of an SAP predefined characteristic is a company's cost centers (technical name: 0COSTCENTER).

Key figure: A numeric value for measuring a business activity (e. g., revenue for a certain month). An example of an SAP predefined key figure is the amount (0AMOUNT).

> **Key figures and queries**
>
>
> In SAP BW, a query always has to contain a key figure.

- *Unit*: Represents the unit (weight, volume, measure, currency, etc.) of a key figure. Examples of an SAP predefined units are the amount units (0UNIT) or currencies (technical name: 0CURRENCY).

- *Time characteristic*: Can be a calendar period (day, month, year), or a certain time. An example of an SAP predefined time characteristic is the fiscal year (technical name: 0FISCYEAR).

> **Time characteristics**
>
>
> Only SAP BW-supplied time characteristics can be used.

- *Technical characteristic*: Used by the SAP BW system. Cannot be defined or changed by the user.

2.3 InfoCubes in brief

InfoCubes ( ) are mainly used for multidimensional reporting (OLAP) and are the primary object used to support queries. They physically store data and are optimized for the performance of queries. The InfoCube data model should be designed after carefully analyzing the business requirements.

2.3.1 InfoCube components

The following components are important for InfoCubes:

- *Characteristics* and *key figures* are as explained for the InfoObjects.
- *Facts* are occurrences of a business activity (e.g., a sale).
- *Dimensions* regroup characteristics that are related.
- *Attributes* provide additional information about characteristics. The address may be an attribute of a client, for example.
- *Granularity* defines the level of detail of the recorded data. For example, data stored at the week level has a lower level of granularity than data stored at the day level.

2.3.2 InfoCube design

An InfoCube is designed as a star schema (see Figure 1.2). The fact table contains the key figures and the dimension IDs. SAP BW uses an *extended star schema* for InfoCubes. The schema is *extended* because the master data used to build the dimension tables to form the unique entries is replaced by keys again. I will go into more detail about this design later.

InfoCubes and dimensions

An InfoCube must contain at least four dimensions. SAP BW automatically assigns three of them: the *data package*, the *time*, and the *unit*. The fourth one must be defined by the user.

InfoCube numbers

The InfoCube schema has the following limitations that must be borne in mind: maximum 16 dimensions; the fact table can contain up to 233 key figures; and 248 maximum characteristics for each dimension.

2.3.3 Four types of InfoCubes

- *Standard InfoCubes* are mainly used and optimized for read access (reporting); InfoCubes can be loaded using the standard loading process.
- *Real-time* InfoCubes are InfoCubes that can be loaded via an interface (APIs). Data is written and read concurrently.
- *VirtualProvider InfoCubes* do not store data; they link to the data in a source system.
- *Semantically partitioned InfoCubes* consist of smaller InfoCubes automatically partitioned by the system. The process is performed for a certain key value, e.g., one InfoCube for each country or for each time period (year).

> **Star schema performance**
>
> A star schema is optimized for fast reading data access. This is possible due to the aggregation of data performed when data is written to the InfoCube and not during the query execution. This is the main aspect of an OLAP system such as SAP BW.

2.4 DataStore Object (DSO) in brief

A *DSO* () stores data in transparent tables. Data is extracted and unified at a very detailed level, and for that reason, DSOs are not optimized for reporting purposes.

2.4.1 DSO components

Key fields and *data fields* are the two types of DSO components. Key fields are InfoObjects that uniquely identify each line. Data fields contain characteristics and key figures loaded from the operational system.

2.4.2 DSO advantages

Using the DSO object provides the following advantages:

- Can be seen as an archive of data from source systems and as the "single point of truth" for the company
- DSO is able to send (e.g., to an InfoCube for reporting) only the data that has been changed instead of the entire set of data received from source systems
- DSO provides more flexibility when, for example, additional data is required due to a change in reporting
- In DSOs, data can be filtered and checked regardless of the layout of the various source systems

2.4.3 DSO and queries

Although I do not recommend creating queries from DSOs, it can be done if required. SAP BW can provide the report-to-report (RRI) interface, which allows a query to jump from InfoCube aggregated data to DSO granular data (drill down).

2.4.4 Types of DataStore Objects

The different types of DSO objects are:

- *Standard DSO:* the most common DSO. It consists of three tables: the *Activation Queue* table contains the recently loaded data, the *Active Data* table contains validated data, and the *Change Log* table keeps track of changes to the active data.
- *Write-optimized DSO:* optimized for fast writing and consist of only the *Active Data* table.
- *Direct update DSO:* as previously described DSO, but the data is loaded using an API interface supplied by SAP BW.
- *In-memory DSO:* the standard DSO that works only with SAP HANA and was introduced in SAP BW 7.3.
- *Semantically partitioned DSO:* the standard DSO partitioned into smaller DSOs according to selected key fields. It was also introduced with SAP BW 7.3.

2.5 MultiProviders in brief

The *MultiProviders* (⚙) combine the data of several InfoProviders and provide a single view of the data. This means that a *union* operation takes place at the database level (see Figure 2.2), combining all values for the InfoProviders.

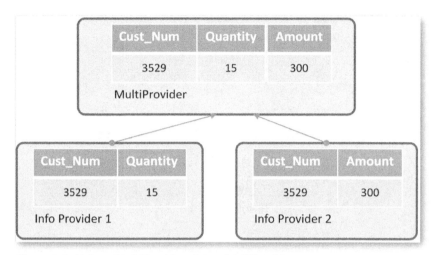

Figure 2.2: Union of InfoProviders into a MultiProvider

MultiProviders do not store data: a query collects data directly from the InfoProviders. To improve the performance of a query, a MultiProvider should preferably be based only on InfoCubes.

2.6 InfoSets in brief

The InfoSets (⚙) do not store data: they combine data from several InfoProviders. They use a *join* operation to display data instead of the *union* operation used by MultiProviders.

> **Data activation**
>
> 👉 By default, only the active (A) version of data is ready for queries. InfoSets are the only objects that allow you to query non-active data in the M (modified) version.

2.6.1 Type of joins for InfoSets

Four types of join operations are available for InfoSets:

- *Inner join:* combines all of the values that have the same reference in both tables (see Figure 2.3). This is the default join operation used by InfoSets.

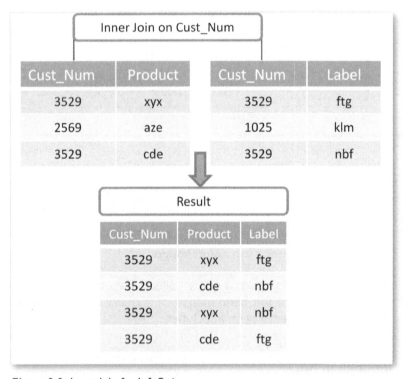

Figure 2.3: Inner join for InfoSets

- *Left outer join* works like an inner join, but includes all values of the left-hand table (see Figure 2.4). The latter is selected by the user.

Left outer join restrictions

Keep in mind that you cannot use an InfoCube as the "right-hand" table of the left join and the right-hand table cannot be joined to another object.

Basic Objects in the SAP BW Layer

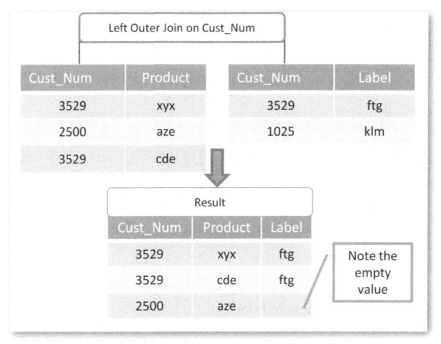

Figure 2.4: Left outer join for InfoSets

- *Temporal join:* available when an InfoSet is created with an InfoProvider that contains an InfoObject with time-dependent attributes. These attributes can be checked against a time characteristic for the other InfoProvider.
- *Anti–join:* returns the values that are present in one InfoProvider but not in the other.

2.6.2 Transitive attribute reporting

InfoSets allow reporting on a second-level attribute. In Figure 2.5, the object *Customer* has the attribute *Sales Representative,* which in turn has its own attribute *City.* Designing the InfoSet with the *Customer* object allows you to navigate to the *City* attribute. The same process is not possible when you design an InfoCube (i.e., you cannot navigate two levels down using an InfoCube).

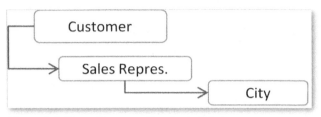

Figure 2.5: Transitive reporting for InfoSets

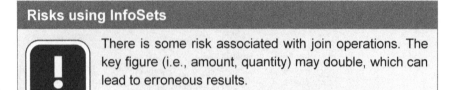

2.7 VirtualProviders in brief

This InfoProvider accesses data in real time directly from a source system. It functions like an InfoCube, except that it does not store any data in the SAP BW system. There are three options for creating a VirtualProvider: 1) based on the data transfer process for direct access; 2) based on a BAPI; 3) based on a function module.

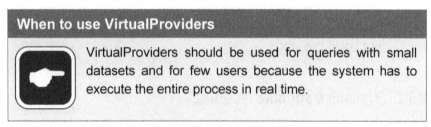

2.8 The Data Warehousing Workbench (DWW)

The DWW is the application used to manage all SAP BW objects. It is launched with transaction code *RSA1,* or via the SAP menu INFORMATION SYSTEMS • BUSINESS INFORMATION WAREHOUSE • MODELING • DATA WAREHOUSING WORKBENCH: MODELING. There are seven sections available at the start of DWW, as shown in Figure 2.6:

BASIC OBJECTS IN THE SAP BW LAYER

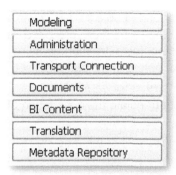

Figure 2.6: The DWW sections

- ▶ The MODELING view contains access to all the objects that can be manipulated in SAP BW (see Figure 2.7):

Figure 2.7: The Modeling section of DWW

- ▶ The ADMINISTRATION section has functions for monitoring the data loading process, remodeling, analyzing, repartitioning, and the process chains tool.
- ▶ The TRANSPORT CONNECTION section allows the transfer of objects from a testing environment to the production system.
- ▶ The DOCUMENTS section allows you to attach documentation to your reports that is accessible to the end users.

29

- ▶ The BI CONTENT section contains predefined objects that cover a wide range of business scenarios. This eliminates the need to create everything from scratch. These objects are marked as DELIVERED (D) and must be activated before they can be used. These objects have a technical name starting with zero (0).
- ▶ The TRANSLATION section helps you to translate the description of each object into different languages.
- ▶ The METADATA REPOSITORY section stores all of the existing relationships between SAP BW objects.

2.9 InfoObjects in detail

Let's take a closer look at InfoObjects (characteristics and key figures) and the options available when you are constructing them. Before going further, we will look at the concepts of the *InfoArea* and the *InfoObjectCatalog*.

2.9.1 InfoArea

InfoAreas (◆) are used to organize SAP objects in groups. They represent the highest level of grouping. As an example, all the objects related to human resources are grouped together under one InfoArea. There may be InfoAreas within an InfoArea.

How do you create an InfoArea?

Run the DWW. The MODELING section opens by default. Clicking on INFOOBJECTS will display the tree of existing INFOAREAS. You can either create a completely new INFOAREA (❶) or add it as a subset of an existing one (❷). Right-click on an empty area for the first option or on the chosen InfoArea for the second option (see Figure 2.8).

Figure 2.8: Creating an InfoArea

2.9.2 InfoObject catalog

InfoObject catalogs (📇) contain InfoArea folders that logically group either characteristics or key figures. They are not mandatory, but they are helpful if you need to maintain or read the data warehouse structure objects. One InfoObject can be assigned to multiple catalogs.

Unassigned characteristics and key figures are stored in the InfoObject Catalogs 0CHANOTASSIGNED and 0KEYNOTASSIGNED respectively, under the InfoArea 0NODESNOTCONNECTED.

How do you create an InfoObject catalog?

Under the MODELING section, in the INFOOBJECTS area, right-click an INFOAREA. From the context menu, select CREATE INFOOBJECT CATALOG. The editing windows will appear—here you can choose the name and type (characteristic or key figure) of the new INFOOBJECT CATALOG. Click on the CREATE icon. Then, you have to activate the object using the ACTIVATE icon ( ). At the end of this process, we will have the following structure (see Figure 2.9):

- ◆ InfoArea for Intro to SAP BW 7.3 book
  - 📇 Char InfoObject Catalog
  - 📇 Key Figure InfoObject Catalog

Figure 2.9: InfoObjects catalog structure

2.9.3 Characteristic InfoObjects

The characteristic InfoObjects (🔳) were introduced in Section 2.2.1 and are typically used to build InfoProviders such as InfoCubes (the fields of InfoCube dimensions are represented by InfoObjects).

Characteristic InfoObjects master data

Characteristic InfoObjects can include additional information called *master data*. There are three types of master data: *attributes, texts,* and *hierarchies*. They are stored in master data tables. It is also possible to load master data from a source system such as SAP ERP. In the next step, we will create a characteristic InfoObject and look at these concepts further.

How do you create a characteristic InfoObject?

We create the characteristic InfoObject in the INFOOBJECT CATALOG (see Figure 2.9). Right-click the catalog and select CREATE INFOOBJECT (see Figure 2.10).

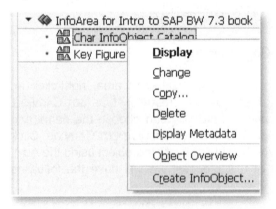

Figure 2.10: Creating a characteristic InfoObject

The CREATE CHARACTERISTIC window opens. Enter the name and long description of the object (see Figure 2.11). In this example, we used a template as an existing object provided by SAP (0COSTCENTER). Our new object will be a copy of the selected template. Clicking on ✅ opens the screen where you can manage the newly created object.

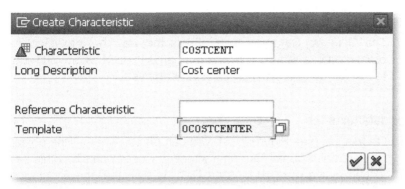

Figure 2.11: Create Characteristic window

2.9.4 Managing the characteristic InfoObject

There are six tabs available for editing the InfoObject (see Figure 2.12):

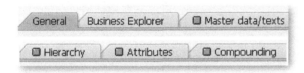

Figure 2.12: Tabs for cost center object

The editing mode for objects is activated by clicking ✏️, the default configuration takes you to the display mode.

General tab

- On the GENERAL tab, the fields LONG DESCRIPTION, DATA TYPE and LENGTH must be completed.
- If you select the ATTRIBUTE ONLY checkbox, the characteristic can only be used as a display attribute for another characteristic and not as navigation attribute. It can be used in DataStore objects, InfoSets, and characteristics as InfoProviders, but cannot be included in InfoCubes.
- The conversion routine (CONVERS. ROUT.) is set to ALPHA for the CHAR type by default. This setting stores the data as follows: if the length of your customer ID is 6, the value 28 is stored as 000028. If a conversion routine is not selected, the system will consider the values 28 and 000028 (or 0028) as different customers.

33

Business Explorer tab

▶ The GENERAL SETTINGS area affects the way the InfoObject is presented in a report. The BEx MAP area is used when you want to include geographical areas in your analysis.

Master data/texts tab

▶ On this tab (see Figure 2.13), you can decide whether the object carries master data. Our characteristic *Cost Center* has this selection active. If WITH MASTER DATA is selected, the ATTRIBUTE tab appears.

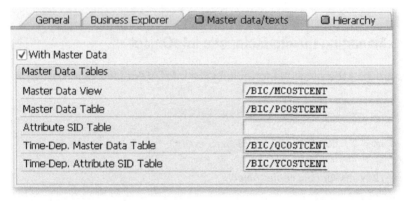

Figure 2.13: Master data activated

▶ The WITH TEXTS option, if selected, will show the descriptive version of a key (useful for analysis and reporting). See Figure 2.14. The SHORT TEXT stores 20 characters and the LONG TEXT stores 60.

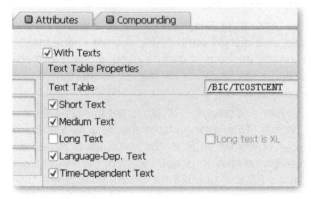

Figure 2.14: With Texts activated

- ▶ The LANGUAGE-DEP. TEXT function translates the text into multiple languages which are shown in queries. The TIME-DEPENDENT TEXT option indicates whether the system should keep the previous value of the modified text with the validity date.
- ▶ The INFOAREA in Figure 2.15 allows the object to be used as an InfoProvider, thus making it available for queries. If you associate the object to an InfoArea, the system checks the option (after saving the changes). You will find the changes in the InfoProvider (· InfoProvider) listed under the MODELING section.

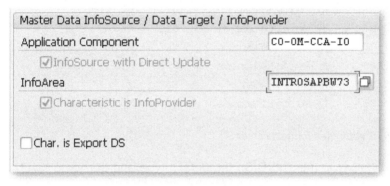

Figure 2.15: Characteristic is an InfoProvider

Hierarchy tab

- ▶ Hierarchies are used to organize data in a parent-child relationship. An example of a hierarchy is *Country-Region-Province-City* (max. 98 levels).
- ▶ You can create multiple versions of the same hierarchy. If, for example, a customer changes cities and you do not want to lose data from the former relationship, activate the checkbox HIERARCHIES, VERSION-DEPENDENT.
- ▶ The TIME-DEPENDENT checkbox defines a period from which the hierarchy is valid.

Attribute tab

- ▶ This tab appears if WITH MASTER DATA was selected on the MASTER DATA/TEXTS tab. Attributes provide additional information about characteristics. Our cost center object carries various attributes (see Figure 2.16).

There are two types of attributes:

▶ NAVIGATIONAL (NAV): similar to a drilldown in a report. SAP queries do not distinguish between characteristics (which are part of InfoCubes) and navigational attributes (not part of InfoCubes). See Figure 2.16.

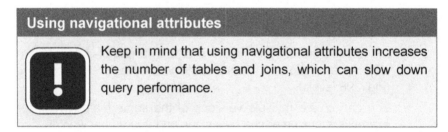

Figure 2.16: Attributes for cost center

▶ DISPLAY ATTRIBUTE (DIS): the default type and the value can be displayed in a report for additional analysis.

> **Using navigational attributes**
>
> Keep in mind that using navigational attributes increases the number of tables and joins, which can slow down query performance.

Attributes of attributes cannot be accessed directly in queries unless objects such as InfoSets are used (see Section 2.6.2).

Compounding tab

▶ The compounding InfoObject is used to reinforce the primary key of the characteristic InfoObject. If there is a risk that the InfoObject value may not be unique for the query, then compounding is necessary to avoid incorrect results in a query. Our COST CENTER object has the controlling area as the compounding object because the same cost center ID may appear in different controlling areas of a company (see Figure 2.17).

BASIC OBJECTS IN THE SAP BW LAYER

Figure 2.17: Compounding tab

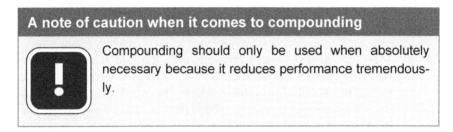

Characteristic InfoObjects and their tables

Activating an InfoObject leads to the creation of the appropriate tables where the individual data values are stored. Based on the selections made on the different tabs, related tables are generated by the system. For our object COST CENTER the following table schema is created (see Figure 2.18).

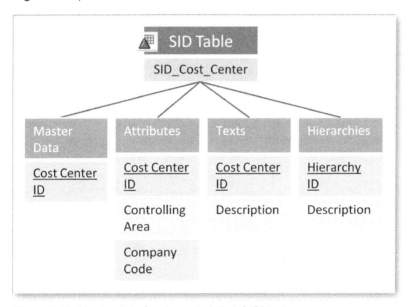

Figure 2.18: Master data for characteristic InfoObject

37

This schema is part of the **extended SAP star schema** used for modeling for InfoCubes (see Section 2.10.1).

Table names
Table names for SAP predelivered objects start with /BI**O**. Objects created by the user generate table names that start with /BI**C**.

- The *SID Table* is always created when the InfoObject is activated, except when the InfoObject is defined as ATTRIBUTE-ONLY on the GENERAL tab. The table contains a numeric ID (an alias) for the characteristic's values. This design improves the performance of the SAP BW system by referring to the ID instead of the characteristics values. Also, the OLAP processor works only with IDs and not with the values directly.

- The *Master Data Table* is created when the WITH MASTER DATA option is selected on the MASTER DATA/TEXTS tab. It includes the characteristics values for the InfoObject.

- The *Text Table* is created when the WITH TEXT option is selected on the MASTER DATA/TEXTS tab. It contains the text values of the characteristic. For example, the *Cafeteria* text corresponds to the cost center ID *1200*. If TIME-DEPENDENT TEXT is selected, the system will also add the fields DATETO and DATEFROM to the table.

- The *Hierarchy Table* is used to store the hierarchical relationships between characteristic values.

- The *Attribute Table* contains the values of the attributes connected to the characteristic InfoObject COST CENTER. For example, it could have values for *business area, company code,* etc.

2.9.5 Key figure InfoObjects

Key figure InfoObjects (🔲) were introduced in Section 2.2.1. They provide a numeric value for a characteristic InfoObject and are significant for the analysis. Amounts and quantities are examples of key figures. We can find them in the fact table of a star schema, along with the dimensions IDs.

How do you create key figure InfoObjects?

Key figure InfoObjects are created in the same way as characteristic InfoObjects (see *How do you create a characteristic InfoObject?* on page 32). The only difference is that you right-click the KEY FIGURE CATALOG instead (see Figure 2.9).

2.9.6 Managing the key figure InfoObject

Once you have created the key figure InfoObject the following tabs are available (see Figure 2.19):

Figure 2.19: Key figure tabs

Type/Unit tab

In this area, you have to assign the type (amount, number, quantity, etc.) and the unit of a key figure (e.g., a currency for the amount). For the AMOUNT, the currency can be fixed (EUR) or flexible. The latter may be the predefined SAP object 0CURRENCY which is responsible for conversion to other currencies (see Figure 2.20).

Basic Objects in the SAP BW Layer

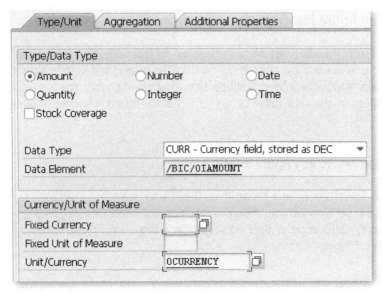

Figure 2.20: The Type/Unit tab

Aggregation tab

- On this tab, you can decide how the key figure will aggregate when presented in a report. The default option is SUM. Table 2.1 explains how the function works.

Cost Center	Period	Amount (€)
1020	January	6000
1020	February	8000
1020	March	5000

Table 2.1: Sum aggregation table

- If we remove the period from the report, the amount is added up by cost center (i. e., 19000 for cost center 1020).
- The EXCEPTION AGGREGATION option makes the aggregation work in a different way. Table 2.2 explains this further:

40

Cost Center	Period	Working Force
1020	January	6
1020	February	6
1020	March	7

Table 2.2: Exception aggregation table

The table contains the number of persons working for cost center 1020 as demonstrated in the working force column. Logically, the number of employees does not add up every month. However, without the EXCEPTION AGGREGATION option selected they do if we remove the period. To avoid an incorrect result, we have to select LAST VALUE from the EXCEPTION AGGREGATION field menu and only the March value is then displayed.

▶ Objects for which it makes no sense to aggregate (e.g., stock inventory) are called non-cumulative values. For those objects, select the NON-CUMULATIVE VALUE option.

Additional Properties tab

This tab adds extra formatting to the key figure type.

2.10 InfoCubes in detail

InfoCubes (🧊) are the main objects used for reporting and analytics purposes. InfoCube design is based on a multidimensional modeling (see Section 1.1.4) implemented in a star schema. SAP has implemented its own schema which we will discuss in further detail.

2.10.1 SAP BW star schema

The SAP BW star schema (see Figure 2.21) is an enhanced version of the classic star schema explained in Section 1.1.5. The InfoObjects that include master data (see *Characteristic InfoObjects and their tables* on page 37) are fundamental to the SAP star schema. In fact, they *extend* the dimension modeling. When activating an InfoObject, SAP BW creates an *SID* table, which contains sequential number IDs linked to the characteristic values of the InfoObject.

Advantages of the SAP BW star schema

▶ A characteristic InfoObject can be used in different InfoProviders and queries at the same time
▶ It is easier to model slow-changing dimensions
▶ Multilingual functionality
▶ Using numerical SIDs keys accelerates access to data

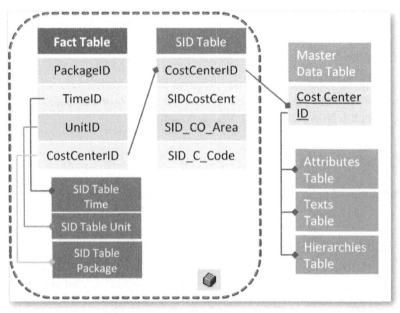

Figure 2.21: InfoCube with SAP extended star schema

2.10.2 Creating an InfoCube

We now have enough information (see Sections 2.3. and 2.10) to start defining an InfoCube.

From the MODELING area of the DWW, select INFOPROVIDER. Right-click the INFOAREA where the InfoCube should go and then choose CREATE INFOCUBE. You have to enter a name and a description. You can also use an existing InfoCube template (from the SAP BI content) to quickly design your own InfoCube.

You then have access to the editing area of the InfoCube (see Figure 2.22). Three default dimensions are created by the system (DATA PACKAGE, TIME, and UNIT) and there must be at least one user-defined dimension (DIMENSION1). To rename DIMENSION 1, right-click it and then choose PROPERTIES from the context menu. New dimensions can be created by right-clicking the DIMENSIONS folder (see Figure 2.23). Do not forget to save your work. When you have completed editing, you can then activate ( ) the InfoCube, which will make it available for queries and reporting activities. The dimensions play a central role in the analyses. Thus, they must be chosen carefully and in line with business requirements.

InfoCube	Techn. name / val...	F...	O.
▼ 🟦 cost center verification	COSTCHECK		
▼ 📘 Object Information			
• 📄 Version	◇ New		🔲
• 📄 Save	⊖ Not saved		
• 📄 Object Status	🟡 Inactive, not ex...		
▸ ⚙ Settings			
▼ 📁 Dimensions			
▸ 🔺 Data Package	COSTCHECKP		
▸ 🔺 Time	COSTCHECKT		
▸ 🔺 Unit	COSTCHECKU		
▸ 🔺 Dimension 1	COSTCHECK1		
▸ 📁 Navigation Attributes			
▸ 📁 Key Figures			

Figure 2.22: Editing an InfoCube

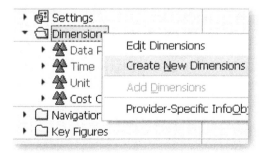

Figure 2.23: New dimension menu

The next step is to integrate the characteristics and key figures into the InfoCube dimensions. To do so, click the INFOOBJECT CATALOG icon (🔳) in the middle column on the InfoCube edit screen. A new window appears: double-click the characteristic catalog we previously created (see Section 2.9.2). The middle column is then filled in with the characteristics and key figures selections made (see Figure 2.24).

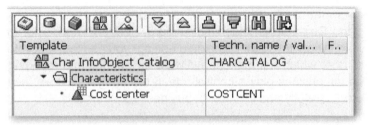

Figure 2.24: Characteristic added to the InfoCube template window

Drag the COST CENTER characteristic into the COST CENTER Dimension. The compounded object CONTROLLING AREA (see Figure 2.25) is also added to the InfoCube structure. You can also fill in dimensions manually. For example, right-click the TIME dimension and choose INFOOBJECT DIRECT INPUT. We will add the SAP predefined fiscal year object 0FISCYEAR (see Figure 2.26).

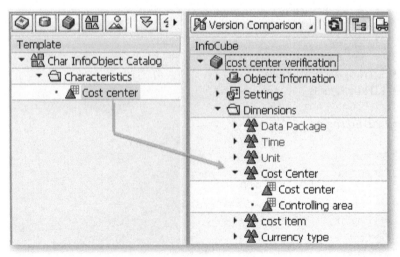

Figure 2.25: Dragging the characteristic into the dimension

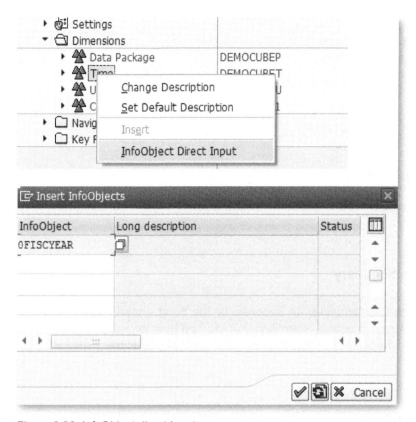

Figure 2.26: InfoObject direct input

The same process can be used to add key figure objects to the KEY FIGURE folder either by using the KEY FIGURE CATALOG INFOOBJECT, or manually from the folder menu.

The folder NAVIGATION ATTRIBUTES contains the attributes associated with the InfoObject characteristics present in the InfoCube (see Figure 2.27). To activate the navigation for the attribute in the InfoCube, select the checkbox ON/OFF.

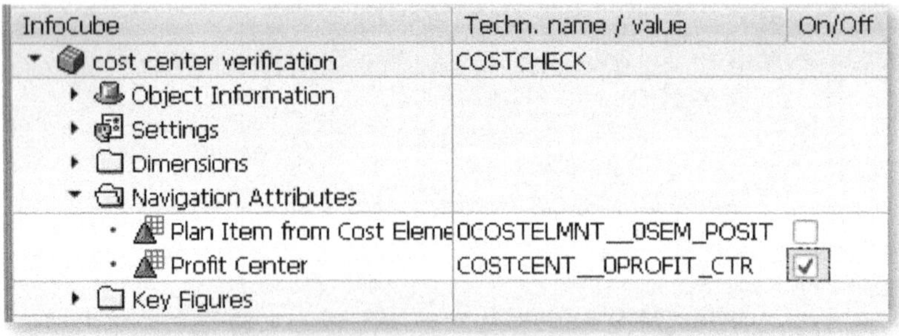

InfoCube	Techn. name / value	On/Off
▼ 🔷 cost center verification	COSTCHECK	
▶ 📦 Object Information		
▶ 🔧 Settings		
▶ 📁 Dimensions		
▼ 📁 Navigation Attributes		
• 📊 Plan Item from Cost Eleme	0COSTELMNT__0SEM_POSIT	☐
• 📊 Profit Center	COSTCENT__0PROFIT_CTR	☑
▶ 📁 Key Figures		

Figure 2.27: Navigation attributes

Activating (🔘) the InfoCube makes it ready for the next step, the ETL process.

2.11 Summary

This chapter provided an overview of the most important SAP BW objects. Using practical examples, you learned how to create an InfoObject and an InfoCube. In the next chapter, we will cover the SAP ETL process.

3 The SAP ETL process

ETL stands for extract, transform, and load (data). It is the process of starting a data transfer from a source system to a destination system. Data from almost any system can be loaded into SAP BW for analytical purposes. This chapter will cover this process from a source system to SAP BW 7.3.

3.1 Extraction

The SAP extraction process (see Figure 3.1) begins with the realization of a **DataSource** (👉) object. For SAP source systems (such as SAP ERP), the object is defined in the source system and is then replicated in BW via the *SAP BI Service API*. For a non-SAP source system, the DataSource is created directly in BW.

DataSource

This object is used to extract data. The **Persistent Staging Area (PSA)** of the DataSource stores the extracted raw data.

After it is created, the DataSource must be activated in order to be available in SAP BW. As a result of the activation, the system creates the PSA table for the DataSource.

PSA (Persistent Staging Area)

Each DataSource activated in SAP BW contains its own PSA.

The PSA represents the entry layer for the BW system. As of SAP BW 7.3, using the PSA table of a DataSource is a required step in the data flow. Afterwards, the data is extracted from the SAP source system to the PSA using the **InfoPackage**. InfoPackages can only load data into a PSA table in *Full Update* mode (all data is transferred) or in *Delta Update* mode (only new data is transferred).

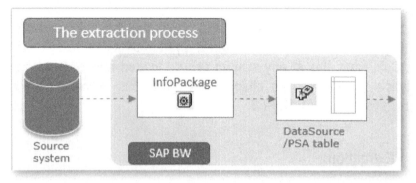

Figure 3.1: The extraction process from a source system

3.1.1 The graphical data flow tool

As of SAP BW 7.3, the DATA FLOWS section has been added to the MODELING area (see Figure 3.2). It is organized into InfoAreas such as INFOPROVIDERS and INFOOBJECTS. InfoAreas include folders for persistent objects (INFOOBJECTS, SOURCE SYSTEMS, and DATASOURCES) and for runtime objects (data transfer process, InfoPackage, and transformations). The graphical data flow tool allows graphical modeling for all objects necessary for the data transfer scenario. A minimal data flow contains a DataSource, a transformation, and an InfoProvider.

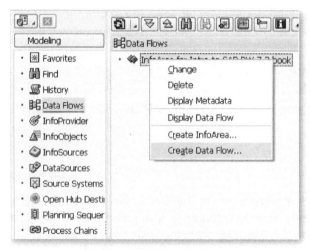

Figure 3.2: Data Flows section

3.1.2 Creating the extraction objects

The extraction process involves the following tasks:

- ▶ Creating a source system
- ▶ Create a DataSource and an application component
- ▶ Create an InfoPackage

Creating a source system

SAP BW supports different types of source systems (see Figure 3.3) accessible from the SOURCE SYSTEMS section of the MODELING area. We will use a flat file source system for our example. To create a file source system, right-click the FILE folder and then choose CREATE.

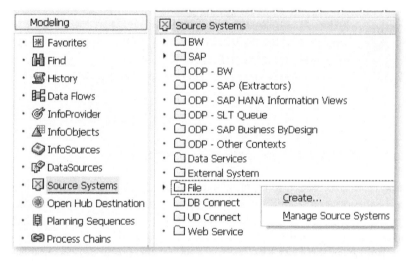

Figure 3.3: Source Systems section

Fill in the fields as shown in Figure 3.4.

Figure 3.4: Creating a file source system

Confirming this action will make the FLAT FILE available under the SOURCE SYSTEMS tree (see Figure 3.5).

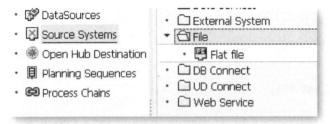

Figure 3.5: Flat file source system (SAP BW screenshot)

> **Using source systems**
>
> When possible, use DB CONNECT or UD CONNECT as a source system. In fact, extracting from a file could lead to many problems (file path, file versioning, field changes) and it is a slow process (the system has to evaluate each line of the file).

Create a DataSource and an application component

The next step is to create a flat file DataSource where you can define the source of the data, the field details, and the data structure. DataSource objects are grouped into *application components*, in the same way that InfoObjects are organized into InfoAreas. To create an application component, right-click the FLAT FILE source system and then choose DISPLAY DATASOURCE TREE (see Figure 3.6).

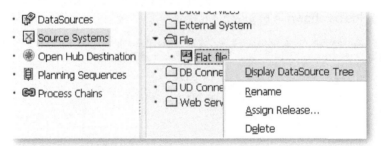

Figure 3.6: Displaying a DataSource tree

This opens the DATASOURCES section where you can create an application component by right-clicking an empty space in the DATASOURCES area (see Figure 3.7). You will need to add a name and a description to create the application component.

Figure 3.7: Creating an application component

Once this step is complete, you have to create the DataSource. Right-click the application component you have just created and then choose CREATE DATASOURCE. The next screen (see Figure 3.8) asks you to provide a unique name and select a DataSource data type:

- ▶ TRANSACTION DATA: data that comes from an operational system and represents a business process (e.g., sales). The data target is either a DSO or an InfoCube.

- ▶ MASTER DATA TEXT: provides descriptive information about data (e.g., customer name). The data target is a characteristic InfoObject configured with text (see *Master data/texts tab* on page 34).

- ▶ MASTER DATA ATTRIBUTES: represent data attributes (such as customer attributes). The data target can be a characteristic InfoObject with master data or a DSO.

In our example, we load attributes from a CSV file into our InfoObject cost center (see Section 2.9.3), thus MASTER DATA ATTRIBUTES must be selected.

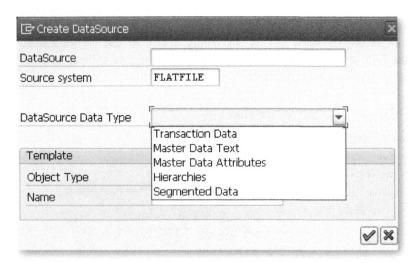

Figure 3.8: Creating a DataSource

The next screen has five tabs where you can configure DataSource properties (see Figure 3.9).

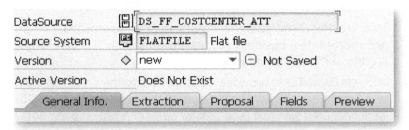

Figure 3.9: DataSource tabs

- GENERAL INFO: Here you can define general information, such as a short, medium, and long description.
- EXTRACTION: Here you can configure the DELTA PROCESS, the DIRECT ACCESS, and the REAL-TIME access (see Figure 3.10). The delta process for flat files provides three options: DELTA ONLY VIA FULL UPLOAD—all records are extracted; FIL0—only new records are extracted and data must first be loaded into a DSO; FIL1—only changed records are extracted.
- For our flat file example, we will select the first option.

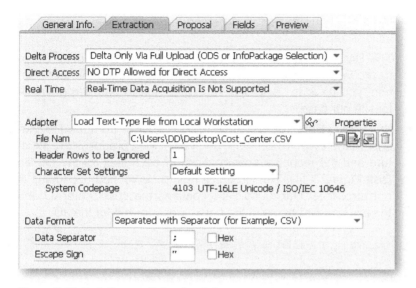

Figure 3.10: DataSource Extraction tab

- The DIRECT ACCESS field allows the configuration of a VirtualProvider based on this DataSource (option ALLOWED). The default setting for a flat file DataSource is NO DTP ALLOWED FOR DIRECT ACCESS. Most of the DataSources do not support direct access.
- With the REAL TIME field you can allow real-time data access from the source system. DataSources based on a flat file do not support real-time extraction.
- With the ADAPTER selections you can provide information about the type and location of data. Our example file is in CSV format located on a local workstation.

Extracting local files

To schedule a background job (and the process chain tool), the file must be saved on the application server.

- You can create a routine for a file name (🖼) if the file name changes regularly. This requires ABAP coding skills.
- Usually, the first row (the header) of a data file contains the column names. You can configure that the first row is ignored by

53

the extraction process by selecting the option HEADER ROWS TO BE IGNORED.

- The DATA FORMAT can be FIXED LENGTH (ASCII files) or SEPARATED WITH SEPARATOR (CSV files). If you choose the latter option, you have to select the separator sign to be used (semicolons in our case).
- PROPOSAL: Here you can LOAD EXAMPLE DATA from the file chosen on the EXTRACTION tab. The system then proposes the structure and the technical specifications of each field for the flat file (see Figure 3.11). This proposal has to be verified because it is not error-free. Our sample file contains the cost center ID and the last and first name of the person responsible for that ID.

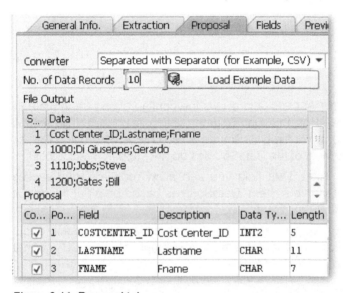

Figure 3.11: Proposal tab

Loading example data

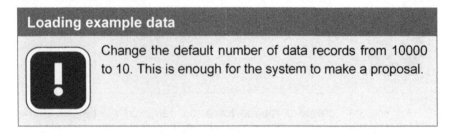

Change the default number of data records from 10000 to 10. This is enough for the system to make a proposal.

▶ FIELDS: This tab (see Figure 3.12) is the place where the Data-Source structure is finalized. The data you find here is the same as the data on the PROPOSAL tab and it can be overwritten. You can decide which field to extract (using the TRANSFER checkbox) and you have to assign each field to an existing InfoObject by completing the column INFOOBJECT TEMPLATE. In our example, we can map the field COSTCENTER_ID to the InfoObject COSTCENT and LASTNAME with 0RESP_PERS (person responsible). This assignment automatically corrects differences in DATA TYPE and LENGTH fields (see Figure 3.13). In fact, COSTCENTER_ID changes to CHAR data type of length 10, and LASTNAME changes the length to 20 instead of the length 11 discovered in our flat file.

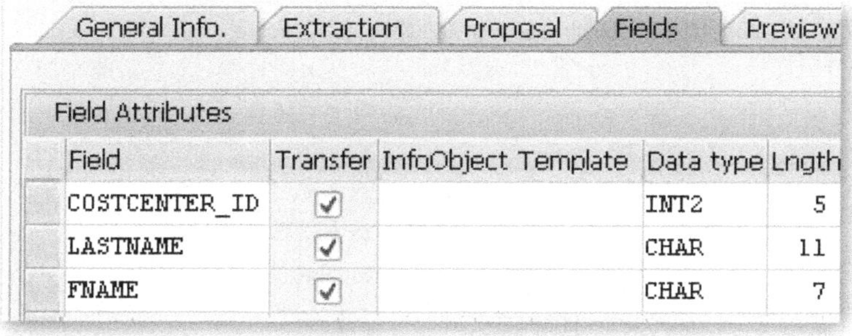

Field Attributes				
Field	Transfer	InfoObject Template	Data type	Lngth
COSTCENTER_ID	✓		INT2	5
LASTNAME	✓		CHAR	11
FNAME	✓		CHAR	7

Figure 3.12: Fields tab (SAP BW screenshot)

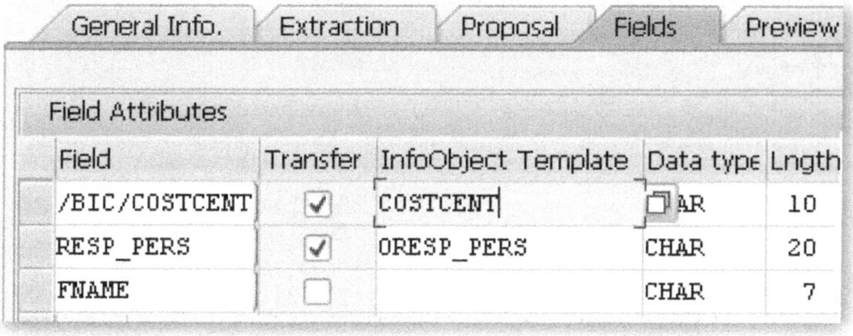

Field Attributes				
Field	Transfer	InfoObject Template	Data type	Lngth
/BIC/COSTCENT	✓	COSTCENT	CHAR	10
RESP_PERS	✓	0RESP_PERS	CHAR	20
FNAME	☐		CHAR	7

Figure 3.13: Mapping of InfoObjects

You can now activate ( ) the DataSource and see a preview of the data on the PREVIEW tab. The activation creates the PSA associated with the DataSource. There is no transformation between the source and the PSA table at this stage.

Create an InfoPackage and extract data

The InfoPackage (▦), when executed, extracts data from a source system to the first layer of SAP BW, the PSA. To create the InfoPackage, open the DATASOURCES section and right-click the newly created DataSource. Select CREATE INFOPACKAGE (see Figure 3.14). On the next screen, you have to enter an InfoPackage description. Clicking on the SAVE button opens the SCHEDULER (MAINTAIN INFOPACKAGE) screen (see Figure 3.15) where the tabs contain mainly the same information as on the DATASOURCE tabs (see Figure 3.9). The extraction phase can be started from the SCHEDULE tab by clicking on the START button. Afterwards, you can monitor the extraction status by clicking the MONITOR icon (▦). Figure 3.16 shows a successful extraction on the STATUS tab. The HEADER tab displays all of the objects involved in this process and the DETAILS tab shows the step-by-step extraction phases.

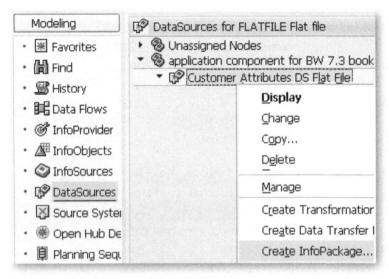

Figure 3.14: Creating an InfoPackage

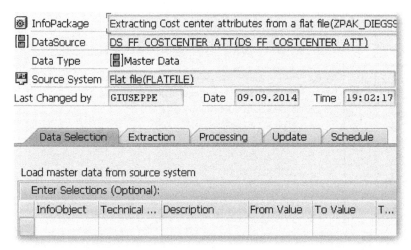

Figure 3.15: InfoPackage tabs

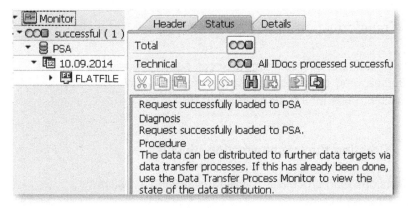

Figure 3.16: InfoPackage monitor

From the MONITOR screen, you can also confirm the data extracted to the PSA. Clicking on the PSA icon (🗃) opens the PSA MAINTENANCE screen where the number of extracted records is displayed by data packet. Click the CONTINUE icon (✓) to view or edit the records (see Figure 3.17). Each line can be edited by double-clicking it.

57

PSA Maintenance

Status	DataP...	Data...	Cost center	Person res	Controlling Area
☐	1	1	0000001000	Di Giuseppe	200
☐	1	2	0000001110	Jobs	210
☐	1	3	0000001200	Gates	220
☐	1	4	0000001210	Page	230
☐	1	5	0000001220	Rubin	240
☐	1	6	0000001230	Filo	250
☐	1	7	0000002100	Codd	260
☐	1	8	0000002200	Ellison	270
☐	1	9	0000002300	Dell	280

Figure 3.17: PSA maintenance

3.2 Transformation

We have defined our data target (cost center), designed the flat file DataSource, and extracted the data to the PSA with the InfoPackage. Now we are ready for the transformation step.

3.2.1 Creating the transformation objects

The transformation process involves the following activities:

- ▶ Making the data target an InfoProvider
- ▶ Creating the transformation object

Making the data target an InfoProvider

To act as a data target, the cost center has to be activated as an InfoProvider. This can be done in two ways:

- ▶ The cost center is activated as CHARACTERISTIC IS INFOPROVIDER (see Figure 2.15)
- ▶ From the INFOPROVIDER section of the MODELING area, right-click the InfoArea concerned then select INSERT CHARACTERISTIC AS INFOPROVIDER (see Figure 3.18) and write the InfoObject name COSTCENT

Both options create the object under the chosen InfoArea in the IN-
FOPROVIDER section (see Figure 3.19).

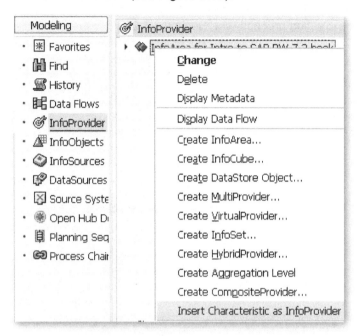

Figure 3.18: Inserting a characteristic as an InfoProvider

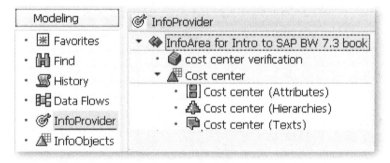

Figure 3.19: Cost center as an InfoProvider

Creating the transformation object

We now have to link the DataSource to the cost center InfoObject (the data target). This is done by creating the object transformation. We want to load attributes data into our data target. Start by right-clicking the COST CENTER (ATTRIBUTES) from the INFOPROVIDER section under the chosen

INFOAREA (see Figure 3.20). Next, select CREATE TRANSFORMATION. The next screen (see Figure 3.21) has the source and target details already populated. The source details are the DATASOURCE and SOURCE SYSTEM created for the extraction process (see Section 3.1.2).

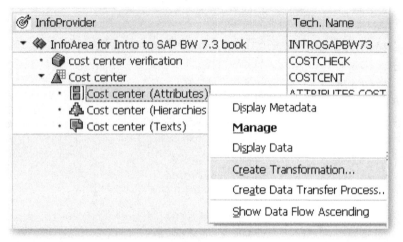

Figure 3.20: Creating a transformation

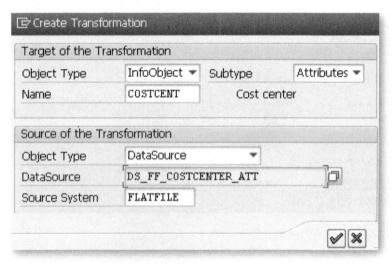

Figure 3.21: Transformation details

Once you have confirmed the transformation details, the TRANSFOR-MATION screen appears (see Figure 3.22).

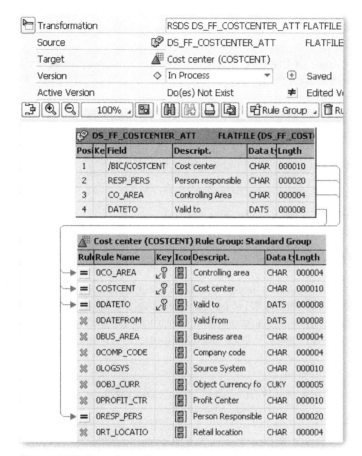

Figure 3.22: Transformation screen

SAP BW automatically matches the DataSource objects to the data target objects. You can change this by dragging and dropping the arrows from the desired source to the destination fields. This type of transformation is known as *direct assignment* because the data is passed from the source to the destination without any change. You are now ready to activate ( ) the transformation. The activation will generate an ABAP program that is executed when you run data loading (DTP).

Activating a transformation

 Only an active transformation can be used during the data loading from the data source to the data target.

61

3.3 Loading

This is the last phase of the ETL process. You load the extracted data from the PSA into the data target object.

3.3.1 Creating the loading objects

The loading process involves the following steps:
- ► Creating the data transfer process (DTP) object
- ► Starting and monitoring the data loading

Creating the DTP (data transfer process)

Activating the transformation created the DTP folder (see Figure 3.23). From here you can create the DTP by right-clicking the folder. The next screen (see Figure 3.24) already contains the required information because you have started the DTP from the transformation directly.

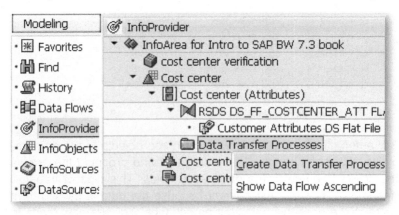

Figure 3.23: Creating the DTP

Confirming the DTP details opens the CHANGE DATA TRANSFER PROCESS screen (see Figure 3.25). We will now discuss the three tabs available on this screen.

- ► EXTRACTION: This tab provides details about the DataSource (our flat file). There are two extraction modes: FULL and DELTA. The full mode loads the entire set of data. The delta mode only loads the new data. The FILTER button allows you to decide which data to load based on your criteria. The SEMANTIC GROUPS button allows the extraction of data records with the same key in the same data package. The PACKAGE SIZE field allows you to select the number of records for each dataset extraction.

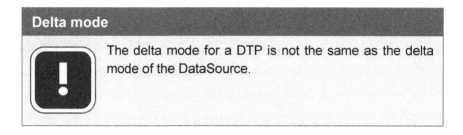

Delta mode

The delta mode for a DTP is not the same as the delta mode of the DataSource.

Package size

Records from DataSources are extracted in a set. After each dataset extraction, the system starts loading into a data target using another process.

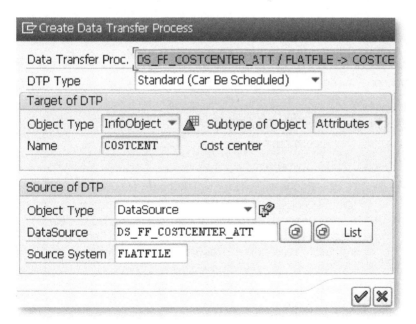

Figure 3.24: DTP information

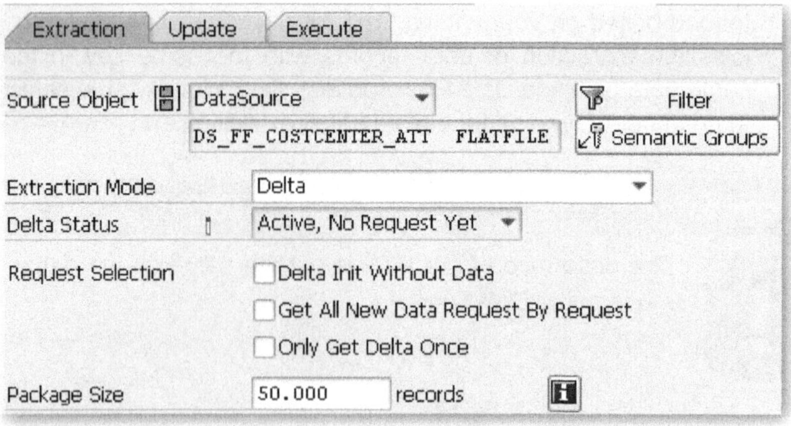

```
┌─ Extraction ─┬─ Update ─┬─ Execute ─┐
                                              
 Source Object [▣] DataSource          ▼         ▽       Filter
                    DS_FF_COSTCENTER_ATT  FLATFILE   ▽ Semantic Groups
 Extraction Mode    Delta                                        ▼
 Delta Status    ⓘ  Active, No Request Yet  ▼
 Request Selection   ☐ Delta Init Without Data
                     ☐ Get All New Data Request By Request
                     ☐ Only Get Delta Once
 Package Size        50.000      records    [H]
```

Figure 3.25: DTP Extraction tab

▶ UPDATE (see Figure 3.26): This tab is primarily used for error handling settings. The first option (CANCEL REQUEST, DO NOT TRACK RECORDS, NO UPDATE) tells the system to suspend the data loading in the case of errors, without writing to an error stack. The second option does the same as the first but tracks the first incorrect record. The REQUEST RED option isolates the erroneous data and loads only valid records into the data target. The REQUEST GREEN option makes the valid data immediately available for reporting.

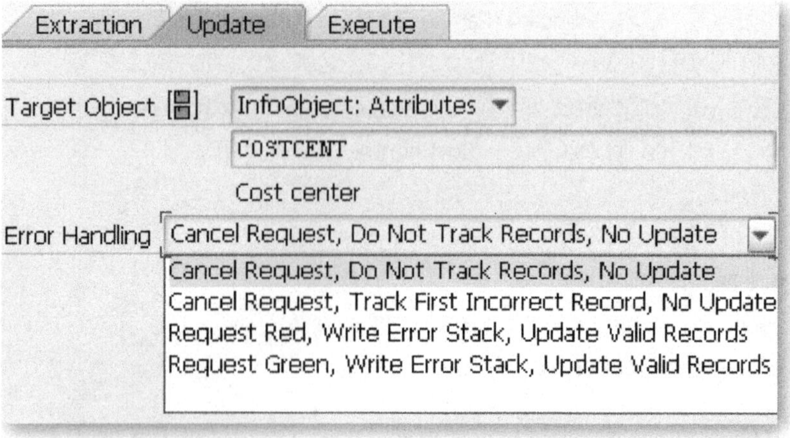

```
┌─ Extraction ─┬─ Update ─┬─ Execute ─┐

 Target Object [▣]   InfoObject: Attributes  ▼
                     COSTCENT
                     Cost center
 Error Handling    Cancel Request, Do Not Track Records, No Update   ▼
                   Cancel Request, Do Not Track Records, No Update
                   Cancel Request, Track First Incorrect Record, No Update
                   Request Red, Write Error Stack, Update Valid Records
                   Request Green, Write Error Stack, Update Valid Records
```

Figure 3.26: DTP Update tab

▶ EXECUTE: This tab allows you to execute the data transfer process by pressing the EXECUTE button. First you have to activate ( ) the DTP. The activation also makes the DTP available in the INFOPROVIDER section, under our INFOAREA (see Figure 3.27).

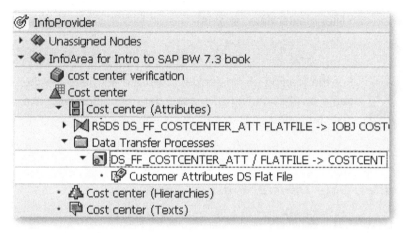

Figure 3.27: DTP activated

Starting and monitoring the data loading

We have just created a DTP that will allow us to load data from the PSA into our data target (cost center). To do so, from the EXECUTE tab of the DTP, press the EXECUTE button (see unterhalb). Click on YES to display the DTP monitor.

Figure 3.28: Executing the DTP

65

A successful data transfer will look like the one shown in Figure 3.29. From the same screen, you can view the transferred data by clicking on the ADMINISTER DATA TARGET icon (👁). The MANAGE INFOPROVIDER screen opens. Select the data target and click on the CONTENTS button (see Figure 3.30). The screen that follows displays all of the attributes where you can filter master data records.

> **Master data text**
>
> For the loading of master data text, the activities are the same as the loading of master data attributes we have just completed.

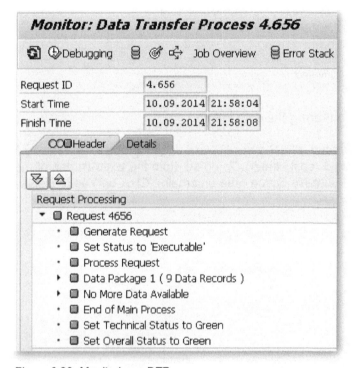

Figure 3.29: Monitoring a DTP

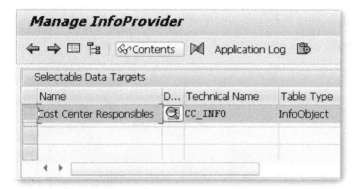

Figure 3.30: Managing InfoProvider content

3.3.2 Creating the ETL with the graphical tool

You can create the exact same ETL process we have just completed graphically from the data flow tool. From the DATA FLOWS section of the MODELING area, right-click an INFOAREA (see Figure 3.2) and then choose CREATE DATA FLOW. A working area opens where you can drag and drop your objects. You have to enter the properties for each object created.

3.4 Recap of the ETL process

We extracted data from an external flat file to an InfoObject data target. Each phase required us to create and set up specific SAP BW objects. A complete view of the ETL process is provided in Figure 3.31.

For the extraction phase we had to create:

- A source system object
- An InfoPackage object
- A DataSource object

The transformation phase included:

- A transformation object

The loading phase has the following object:

- A data transfer process (DTP)

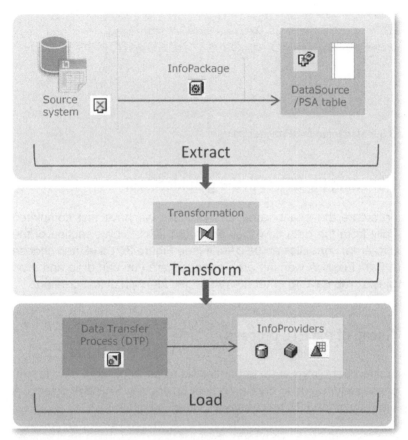

Figure 3.31: An overview of the ETL process

3.5 Summary

In this chapter you learned about the ETL process and how to leverage it in SAP BW. We will now take a look at administration tools and process chains.

4 Administration tools and process chains

In this chapter, we will look at the administration of InfoCubes and DataStore objects. We will also learn how to automate ETL flow tasks using process chains.

4.1 The administration functions

All the administration functions in SAP BW 7.3 are grouped under the ADMINISTRATION section of the DWW (see Figure 4.1). This section can also be accessed by executing transaction RSMON.

Figure 4.1: Administration section

4.1.1 Overview of the administration functions

We will now explain each administration function briefly:

PROCESS CHAINS: The goal of process chains is to execute repetitive processes automatically according to predefined rules.

ADMINISTRATION COCKPIT: This function is used to verify the global status and performance of the business warehouse.

MONITORS: All main tasks performed by the SAP system are grouped under the MONITORS function. Figure 4.2 provides an overview of the specific tasks you can monitor.

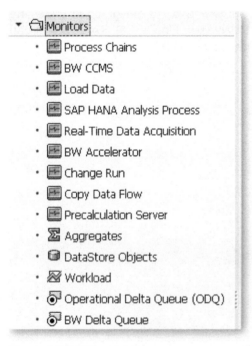

Figure 4.2: Monitors panel

CHANGE RUN: Loading new master data may result in changes to attributes or hierarchies. In order to keep the reporting results consistent, you have to adjust the data by executing a CHANGE RUN.

> **Active and modified versions**
>
> Master data and hierarchies are recorded in two versions: the active version (can be used in queries) and the modified version. If there are changes to master data, they are not available for reporting until you execute the *change run*.

BROADCASTING: Broadcasting allows the distribution of queries and reports to various channels. It can be scheduled periodically or on predefined dates.

ANALYSIS AUTHORIZATIONS: This function allows you to control and set up user access to BW transactions. It is also accessible using transaction code RSECADMIN.

METADATA SEARCH: With this function, you can assign documents to BW objects to better describe their use and function.

MIGRATION 3.X OBJECTS: This tool provides what is required to migrate objects only available in SAP BW 3.x to SAP BW 7.x. This tool is also accessible using transaction code RSMIGRATE.

REMODELING: This tool allows you to create remodeling rules to facilitate automatic changes to the structure of InfoCubes (without losing data) and DSO objects.

> **InfoCubes and remodeling**
>
> When you want to change the structure of an InfoCube, you usually have to delete all the data in it. Remodeling helps to prevent this by allowing you to create remodeling rules.

REPARTITIONING: To improve access (read and write) operations for an InfoCube, you have to fragment tables regularly. Repartitioning facilitates this task.

MASS ACTIVATION OF BADI SPOS: SAP BW 7.3 introduced SPOs (semantically partitioned objects). The partitioning can be done either manually, or, using this function, automatically.

ANALYSIS OF BI OBJECTS: This function allows you to test the technical consistency of various BW objects.

Analysis of BI objects

 This analysis consists of a technical verification and therefore will not identify any faults related to the business logic.

CURRENT SETTINGS: This folder has several transactions from which you can perform basic SAP BW settings (see Figure 4.3).

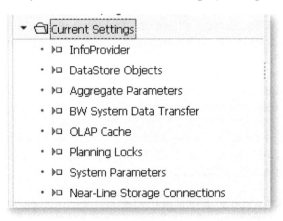

Figure 4.3: Current settings

4.2 Managing InfoCubes

The administration of an InfoCube can be performed from one single place. Right-click an InfoCube and select MANAGE (see Figure 4.4). The ADMINISTRATION screen appears.

Six tabs are available for executing the InfoCube administrative tasks (see Figure 4.5).

Administration Tools and Process Chains

Figure 4.4: Managing an InfoCube

Contents	Performance	Requests	Rollup	Collapse	Reconstruction
Dimensions with InfoObject for InfoCube:cost center verification(COSTCHECK)					
Description	InfoObject	Dimension Name	Dimension		
Change Run ID	0CHNGID	Data Package	COSTCHECKP		
Record type	0RECORDTP	Data Package	COSTCHECKP		
Request ID	0REQUID	Data Package	COSTCHECKP		
Fiscal year	0FISCYEAR	Time	COSTCHECKT		
Fiscal year variant	0FISCVARNT	Time	COSTCHECKT		
Currency key	0CURRENCY	Unit	COSTCHECKU		
Controlling area	0CO_AREA	Cost Center	COSTCHECK1		
Cost Element	0COSTELMNT	cost item	COSTCHECK2		
Currency Type	0CURTYPE	Currency type	COSTCHECK3		

Figure 4.5: InfoCube tabs

73

CONTENTS: This tab displays all the characteristics objects assigned to the InfoCube and the dimension to which they belong (see Figure 4.5). In addition, there are three buttons provided at the bottom of the screen:

INFOCUBE CONTENT: Pressing this button calls up the screen where you can select the filters and the fields for the characteristics you want to view.

FACT TABLE: Pressing this button allows you to view the fact table content based on the dimensions keys and key figures.

DELETE SELECTION: With this function you can delete data records based on certain criteria.

> **Deleting data from an InfoCube**
>
> Great care must be taken when executing the deletion operation because it can have a serious impact on the BW data integrity. A more secure way is to delete data using the archiving process.

PERFORMANCE: This tab proposes different options for improving the data loading process for the InfoCube (see Figure 4.6). On the upper part of the screen (DB INDEXES), you can optimize indexes to speed up access to the InfoCube data. Using the buttons on the lower part of the screen (DB STATISTICS), you can improve query performance.

REQUESTS: Every time data is loaded into the InfoCube, the BW system generates a unique request ID.

From this tab, you can manage and monitor all of the requests for this InfoProvider.

ROLLUP: With this function, you can update aggregates that are defined for the InfoCube. We will cover aggregates in further detail in Chapter 6.

COLLAPSE: This function (see Figure 4.7) provides compression functionality for InfoCubes. The compression process consolidates data loaded after removing the *request ID*. The data load is usually performed periodically and as time goes on, the fact table continues to grow.

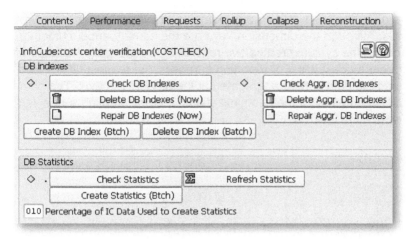

Figure 4.6: Performance tab

Figure 4.7: Collapse tab

> **Fact table and query performance**
>
> 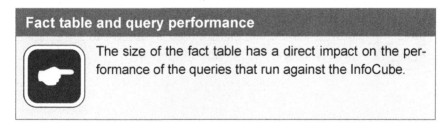 The size of the fact table has a direct impact on the performance of the queries that run against the InfoCube.

To understand the benefits of compression, it is important to realize how data is loaded into the fact table. Figure 4.8 shows a simple load of two

75

data records executed at different moments and thus with different request IDs. Although the dimension keys are the same (period, customer, and product) the system creates two records in the fact table because of the different request IDs. For reporting purposes, the request ID is superfluous and the data can be aggregated at the amount (€) level. The compression executes all of these optimizations, thereby creating a new fact table (see Figure 4.9).

Fact Table (F) — **Before** compression

Request ID	Period	Customer	Product	€
1956	092014	75	004	200
1957	092014	75	004	150

Figure 4.8: New data loaded into the fact table

Fact Table (E) — **After** compression

Period	Customer	Product	€
092014	75	004	350

Figure 4.9: The fact table after compression

Two fact tables

New data is first loaded into the *F* fact table of the InfoCube. After compression, data is moved into the *E* fact table and data in the F table is *deleted*.

Start a compression from the COLLAPSE tab (see Figure 4.7) and enter the request ID. All requests previous to the chosen one (included) are compressed. Clicking the RELEASE button starts the compression process.

RECONSTRUCTION: This tab is used to restore a deleted request for InfoCubes that use the 3.x data flow model.

Reconstruction

To use the reconstruction function, the data loaded into the InfoCube 3.x must be present in the PSA of the DataSource or the DataStore.

4.3 Managing a DataStore (DSO)

In Section 2.4, we took our first look at the primary DSO characteristics. We will now learn how to create and manage a DSO.

SAP BW design

It is design best practice to use a DSO that keeps operational data from various sources before transferring data to InfoCubes or data targets.

4.3.1 Creating a DSO

From the MODELING area of the DWW, go to the INFOPROVIDER section and right-click the INFOAREA that the DSO should belong to. From the context menu, select CREATE DATASTORE OBJECT. On the next screen, provide a name and a description for the DSO. Confirming these settings opens the EDIT DATASTORE OBJECT screen (see Figure 4.10).

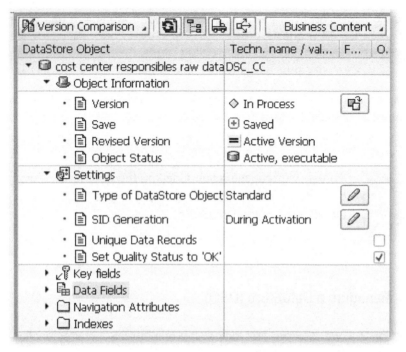

Figure 4.10: Editing a DSO

The DSO needs to know which data will be loaded (DATA FIELDS) and what the KEY FIELDS are that uniquely identify a record. To provide this information, use the same procedure as used for the InfoCube dimensions (see Section 2.10.2).

After selecting the data fields and key fields, you can activate your DSO. From the SETTINGS folder, choose the DSO type (STANDARD, DIRECT UPDATE, or WRITE-OPTIMIZED) and the SID GENERATION.

DSO type and SID generation

 Write-optimized DSOs are a better solution for improving the overall performance of the SAP BW system. Do not use *SID Generation* if the DSO is not meant to be used for reporting.

4.3.2 Loading data to a DSO

The data transfer from a source system to a DSO follows the same ETL process as explained in Chapter 3. Refer to Section 3.4 for a quick refresher.

4.3.3 Managing a DSO

After the data load, you can start the administrative tasks associated with DSO. Right-click your DSO and select MANAGE. The MANAGE INFOPROVIDER screen opens. You can use the following three tabs to manage this object:

CONTENTS: This tab contains the list of InfoObjects present in the DSO tables. As you can see from Figure 4.11, an object called 0RECORDMODE has been added to the list by the BW system. This InfoObject is used internally by the system and is added to the three tables for the standard DSO.

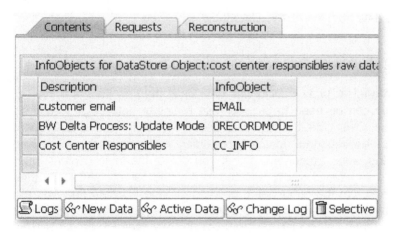

Figure 4.11: DSO contents tab

From the CONTENTS tab, you can also manage the three tables created for a standard DSO: the ACTIVATION QUEUE table (accessible via the NEW DATA button), the ACTIVE DATA table (ACTIVE DATA button), and CHANGE LOG table (CHANGE LOG button).

Standard DSO data activation process

After successful data loading, data is first stored in the ACTIVATION QUEUE table. The ACTIVATION QUEUE table consists of the data loaded plus three technical keys added by the system: the REQUEST SID, the PACKAGE ID, and the RECORD NUMBER. The data will be available for reporting or for other InfoProviders after it is activated from the REQUESTS tab (see Figure 4.13). The activation moves data to the ACTIVE DATA table. The technical keys are removed and the primary table key is the one chosen during the DSO creation. The data is now available. All modifications to records with the same key fields are stored in the CHANGE LOG table.

DSO types

Write-optimized and *direct update* DSOs only have the ACTIVE DATA table.

Deleting DSO data

You can delete specific DSO records by clicking the SELECTIVE button. Only the data from the ACTIVE DATA table is deleted.

Deleting change log data

The CHANGE LOG table is filled with data once the new data is activated. This table can be used to provide data for other data targets such as InfoCubes. Over time, the table can become quite large due to frequent changes. An important maintenance task is to regularly delete the change log table. I recommend that you delete the table content when the data has been correctly updated to the data targets and some time has passed. On the other hand, deleting change log data removes the historical changes to the data. To delete log data, go to the ENVIRONMENT menu and then select DELETE CHANGE LOG DATA (see Figure 4.12). This task can also be automated using process chains.

ADMINISTRATION TOOLS AND PROCESS CHAINS

Figure 4.12: Deleting change log data

REQUESTS: This tab displays similar information to the INFOCUBE REQUESTS tab (see Figure 4.13).

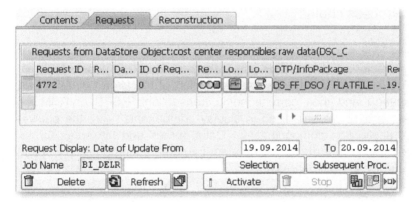

Figure 4.13: DSO requests tab

Each line represents a unique request that occurred for the DSO. You can DELETE a request and ACTIVATE the data.

> **Deleting a request and activating data**
>
> 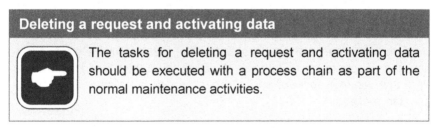 The tasks for deleting a request and activating data should be executed with a process chain as part of the normal maintenance activities.

Before deleting a request (that probably contains incorrect data), you should verify whether these two conditions are satisfied:

81

1. If the wrong data has already been transferred to further data targets, this must be deleted as well.
2. If there are newer requests than the one you want to delete, they must be deleted first because they may contain dependent data from the request.

RECONSTRUCTION: This tab provides the opportunity to reload DSO data that has been transferred using the 3.x data flow. From the BW 7.x version, it is sufficient to execute the DTP for reloading, making this tab pointless.

4.4 Process chains

Process chains help to automate most of the SAP BW recurring tasks, saving precious time for SAP administrators. They are accessible from the MODELING or the ADMINISTRATION section of the DATA WAREHOUSING WORKBENCH and their corresponding transactions RSPC or RSMON. Process chains are organized in display components ( ), the equivalent of application components for DataSources and InfoAreas for InfoObjects. Create a display component by right-clicking an empty space in the PROCESS CHAINS area.

4.4.1 Creating a process chain

In this section, we will learn how to automate the ETL process from the extraction phase to the loading of data into a data target. You can start the process chain creation process by right-clicking the display component where the process belongs and selecting CREATE PROCESS CHAIN. Confirm with a name and a description. The INSERT START PROCESS window then appears (see Figure 4.14). Click the CREATE icon. The START PROCESS window appears and you can provide a meaningful name for the start process.

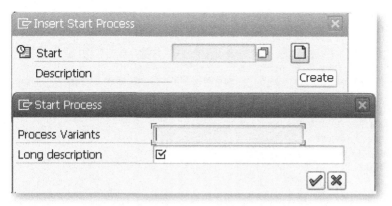

Figure 4.14: Starting a process chain

Confirming your entries opens the MAINTAIN START PROCESS screen (see Figure 4.15) where you can decide on the process scheduling options by clicking the CHANGE SELECTIONS button.

Figure 4.15: Maintaining the start process

Save your settings and click the back button ⬅ to return to the PROCESS CHAIN MAINTENANCE screen (see Figure 4.16). On the right-hand panel you see the newly created start object. On the left-hand panel you see the list of all objects that you can include in the process chain flow.

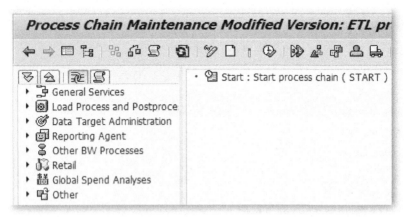

Figure 4.16: Process chain maintenance

The first process to include in the process chain is the execution of the data extraction from a source system (see Figure 3.31 for an overview of the ETL process), which is realized by the InfoPackage. Click on LOAD PROCESS AND POSTPROCESSING and drag and drop EXECUTE INFOPACKAGE into the right-hand panel. This opens the INSERT EXECUTE PACKAGE screen, where you can select an existing InfoPackage or create a new one (see Figure 4.17).

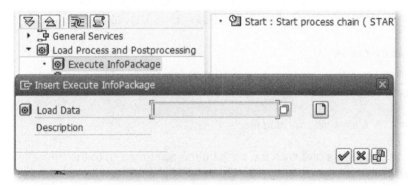

Figure 4.17: Inserting Execute InfoPackage

If you choose an existing InfoPackage that is already part of an ETL data flow (i.e., you have already defined all the objects), the next window shows all the InfoObjects related to the data flow (see Figure 4.18) with the correct links between the objects. You only have to link the START PROCESS with EXECUTE INFOPACKAGE by dragging and dropping from the first object to the second one. Our example automates a DSO load from a flat file.

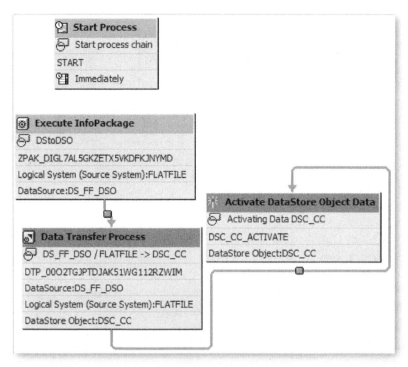

Figure 4.18: Process chain flow

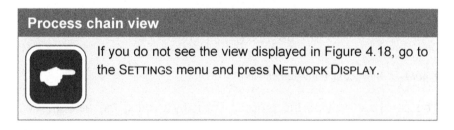

You can check the process chain by clicking the CHECKING VIEW button (🔍). This action should display the process chain as shown in Figure 4.19, confirming that all of the steps are error-free.

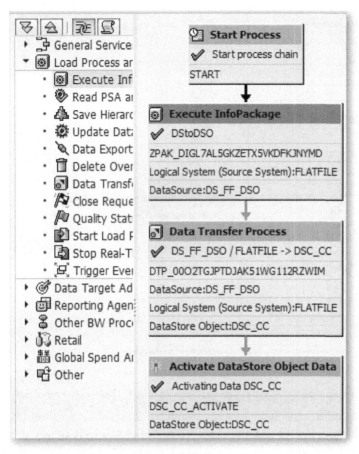

Figure 4.19: Process chain check view

You can now activate the process chain by clicking the activate icon ( ).

4.4.2 Managing a process chain

Managing a process chain consists of executing and monitoring the process. To start the execution, press the SCHEDULE icon ( ). The execution will run according to your scheduled option (see the CHANGE SELECTIONS button in Figure 4.15). To monitor the execution, click the LOG VIEW icon ( ). The screen shown in Figure 4.20 appears.

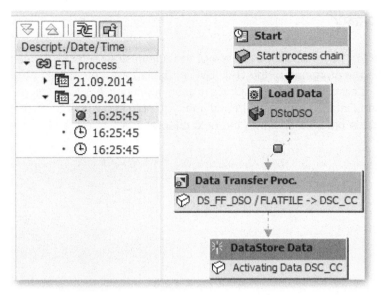

Figure 4.20: Process chain log

The process shows an error during the InfoPackage (⚙) load. This has happened because in our example scenario, the source data is located on a local workstation. Transferring the data to an application server will solve the issue.

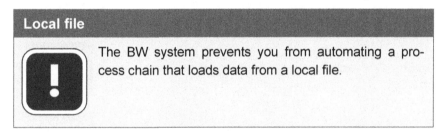

Setting alert messages

You may want to receive an alert so that you know the result of one or all of the process chain steps. To do so, right-click one of the objects and then select CREATE MESSAGE. Flag the action that you want to receive a message for (successful, errors, or always). Give your message a title. You can then choose EDIT DOCUMENTS or to MAINTAIN RECIPIENT LIST. Once you have edited the content of the message and the recipient list, the message is included as a step in the process chain for the object from which it was created.

4.5 Summary

In this chapter, I provided an overview of the administrative tasks necessary for the maintenance of the SAP BW infrastructure. You should now have an understanding of the administration functions required for InfoCubes and DataStore objects. In addition, you now know how to create and manage a process chain. In the next chapter, we'll take a look at BI Content.

5 SAP BI Content

This chapter introduces you to the components of SAP BW Business Content (BI Content). Using it can accelerate the design process for your BW objects. We will also introduce the Metadata Repository.

5.1 The purpose of BI Content

Many objects are used in SAP BW to analyze company data. Defining objects from scratch represents a huge amount of work and high costs for the IT department. SAP BI Content addresses this issue by providing predefined objects that are ready to use. Thus, you should always check the BI Content before defining BW objects. The BI Content objects can be activated and used as provided or adapted to the company's requirements.

> **BI Content objects**
>
> The BI Content objects do not contain any data and are simply predefined structures of BW objects.

The content provided by SAP BW is suitable for general business scenarios, specific scenarios, and also for specific industries (e.g., healthcare, media, high tech, and automotive). For a complete list of industry-specific solutions, refer to *www.sap.com/solution.html*.

5.2 Overview of BI Content objects

BI Content is accessible from the DWW or using transaction code RSORBCT. The objects available are displayed in the OBJECT TYPES list shown in Figure 5.1.

Roles

Common business roles, with preconfigured authorizations, are also part of the BI Content. They can be found under the ROLES list as shown in Figure 5.2. The roles are mostly grouped by industry type. Activating a role gives access to all groups of objects required for that particular job (e.g., InfoProviders, DataSources, reports). Just like any other BI Content object, the roles can be modified to meet specific requirements within in a company.

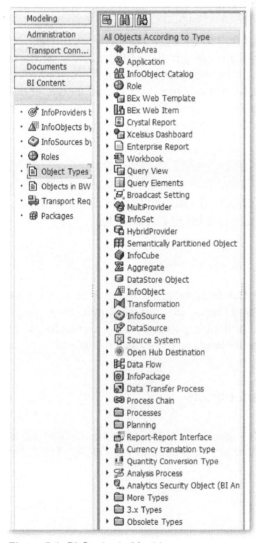

Figure 5.1: BI Content object types

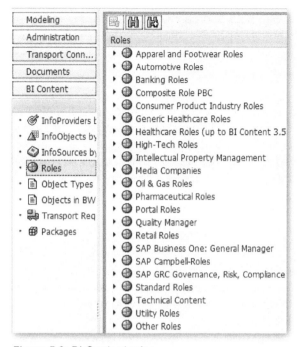

Figure 5.2: BI Content roles

Packages

BI Content also provides ready-to-use business packages. They contain all of the objects required for specific business process reporting. The packages serve as analytical applications and are used in combination with an operational system such as ERP or CRM.

5.3 Versions of the BI Content objects

In the BW system, the BI Content objects may have three versions at same time: delivery (D), modified (M), and active (A).

Delivery version

The initial version of the BI Content objects is the delivery (D) version. When SAP provides an update or new release for BI Content objects, only the D version objects are taken into consideration. The D version objects cannot be loaded with data and cannot be used in any model at all. The D version objects are under SAP control.

Modified version

This version is assigned to BI Content objects installed and transferred from the D version. It is also assigned if you make changes to an active version object. Only metadata modifications are considered as changes and thus, new data loaded to an active version object does not change the object version. The changes only take effect after the modified object is activated.

Active version

Only the objects that have an A version can be used in the BW system and can be transported between BW systems. The A version is assigned to the object when it is activated. Activating a D or an M object leads to a change to an A version of that object.

A and M versions
The A and M versions are copies of the D version. Users can use them as delivered, or can modify them. Thus, those versions are under the control of the user.

5.4 Activating BI Content objects

BI Content objects must be activated prior to their use in the BW system. This process is simplified thanks to the BI Content graphical interface. Objects can first be filtered by the categories shown on the left-hand panel in Figure 5.3.

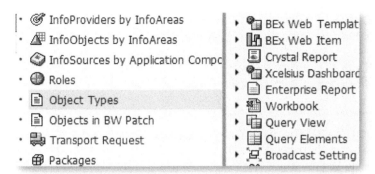

Figure 5.3: Object categories

Based on that selection, you will have different views of the available objects ready to be installed from the SAP system. For example, the OBJECT TYPES category will be displayed as shown in Figure 5.1. This is the first step of the activation process. The second one consists of choosing the object you want to install and defining some settings.

Grouping and collection settings

Before proceeding with the activation of an object, you have to tell the system how you want to consider the other objects that are relevant for your selected object. For example, if you install an InfoCube, you may want to also install the InfoObjects that belong to it. This is possible using the GROUPING functionality settings.

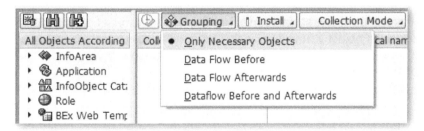

Figure 5.4: Grouping functionality

The default option is ONLY NECESSARY OBJECTS, which collects only the minimum objects necessary for the activation.

93

The option DATA FLOW BEFORE additionally includes objects that provide data (e.g., DataSources) to the selected object.

The option DATA FLOW AFTERWARDS also activates the objects that receive data from the selected object (e.g., queries based on the InfoCube).

The last option, DATAFLOW BEFORE AND AFTERWARDS, is a combination of the previous two options and it is the maximum transfer of objects you can get from the BI Content.

The COLLECTION MODE functionality has two options (see Figure 5.5). The COLLECT AUTOMATICALLY option tells the system to start the collection of dependent objects immediately.

The START MANUAL COLLECTION option allows you to manually select the objects to be activated.

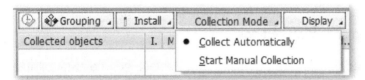

Figure 5.5: Collection mode options

Choosing the object to install

After selecting the first category from the left-hand panel, you have to select which object you want to install from the middle panel. To install an InfoCube, we first select the OBJECT TYPES category then expand the INFOCUBE object from the middle panel (see Figure 5.6).

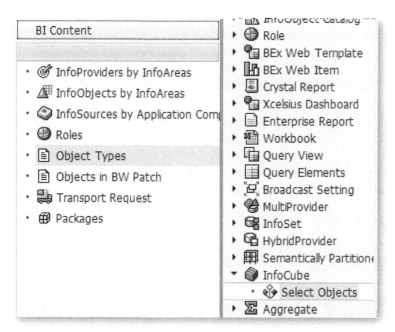

Figure 5.6: InfoCube selection

Now double-click SELECT OBJECTS. This opens a window with all of the InfoCubes available for installation (see Figure 5.7). Double-clicking the chosen object will make it available in the right-hand panel of the BI Content (see Figure 5.8). All related objects are included in the InfoCube structure. The INSTALL column is checked automatically by the SAP system if the object is not yet active in the BW environment. These selected objects are the ones that will be transferred during the activation process.

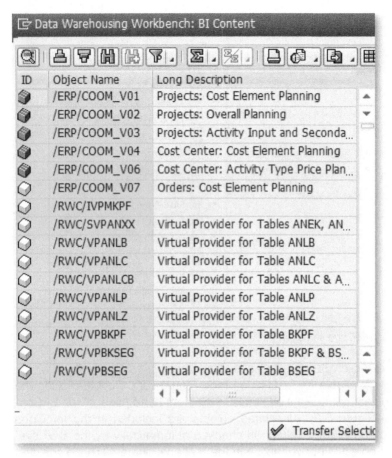

Figure 5.7: InfoCube BI Content

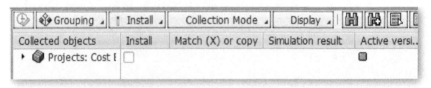

Figure 5.8: Selected BI Content object

The MATCH (X) OR COPY column is checked by the system if an object has a new SAP release and this is already active in the BW system. In this scenario, you have three possible selections:

1. You can deselect the INSTALL and MATCH(X) OR COPY checkboxes for the object concerned. In that case, the new SAP object release is ignored during the activation.

2. You can deselect the MATCH(X) OR COPY checkbox for the object concerned. The system will then overwrite (without a merge) the existing object with the new object release. All modifications made to the existing object will be lost.

3. You can leave the two options selected. The system will try to merge the existing object with the new object released by SAP. If there is no automatic match, the system will ask which properties should be transferred.

Object merge

 Not all of the BW objects can be merged, for example transformations and queries cannot be merged. In that case, the system overwrites the existing object version with its new released version.

The ACTIVE VERSION AVAILABLE column (see Figure 5.8) tells us that the object is already active in our BW system and the object does not have a new release available from SAP.

Executing the activation

Once all of the previous settings have been decided, we can proceed to install (or to activate) the BI Content objects. The INSTALL functionality provides four options (see Figure 5.9):

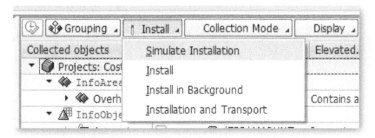

Figure 5.9: BI Content installation options

The SIMULATE INSTALLATION option tests whether errors could occur during the activation. The result is shown under the SIMULATION RESULT column (see Figure 5.8).

The INSTALL option processes the activation immediately. The objects are ready to use if no errors were detected.

The INSTALL IN BACKGROUND option is used when a large number of objects have to be activated.

The INSTALL AND TRANSPORT option activates and writes the objects to a transport request.

A successful activation makes the objects ready to use in the DWW InfoProvider tree.

5.5 Metadata Repository

The Metadata Repository is the place where you can find information about the BW objects that are active in the system or are part of the BI Content. This functionality is accessible from the DWW (see Figure 5.10).

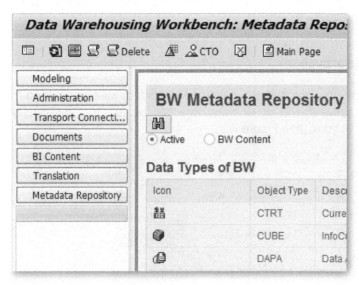

Figure 5.10: Metadata Repository

The Metadata Repository can be regarded as the catalog of BW objects and it also contains the relationships between individual objects.

5.5.1 Using the Metadata Repository

From the initial screen (see Figure 5.10), you can select to search ACTIVE objects or BW CONTENT objects. Then double-click an object, for instance an InfoCube. A list containing all active InfoCubes appears. Double-clicking one InfoCube calls up the screen shown in Figure 5.11. The top part of the screen contains generic descriptions for the selected object.

At the bottom of the screen you will find information about the related objects classified on the following tabs (see Figure 5.12). The REQUIRED OBJECTS tab contains the objects used to build the InfoCube. The USED BY tab contains all other objects that use the InfoCube. The tabs IN PREVIOUS DATA FLOW and IN SUBSEQUENT DATA FLOW contain objects that are positioned before (e.g., transformations, DTP) and after (MultiProviders, Queries) a data flow respectively.

Figure 5.11: Metadata description

Object in Environment				
Required Objects	Used by	In Previous Data Flow		In Subsequent Data Flow
Icon	Name	Description (Short)	Description (Long)	
	/ERP/AMOUNT	Amount	Amount	
	/ERP/COSTELMT	Cost Element	Cost Element	
	/ERP/CO_AREA	Controlling Area	Controlling Area	
	/ERP/CURTYPE	Currency Type	Currency Type	
	/ERP/METYPE	Key Figure Type	Key Figure Type	
	/ERP/PARTACTY	Sender Activity Type	Sender Activity Type	
	/ERP/PARTCCTR	Sender Cost Center	Sender Cost Center	

Figure 5.12: Metadata object environment

The DISPLAYED IN tab shows which InfoArea the object belongs to, and finally, the OBJECT DETAILS tab provides the option of displaying the object data flow and the InfoCube star schema graphically. Those tabs become visible (see Figure 5.13) by selecting one of the following icons .

Object in Environment			
	Displayed in	Object Details	
Icon	Name	Description (Short)	Description (Long)
	/ERP/COOM	Overhead Cost Contro	Overhead Cost Controlling

Figure 5.13: DISPLAYED IN and OBJECTS DETAILS tabs

5.6 Summary

In this chapter, I presented the preloaded SAP BI objects gathered by the SAP BI Content. You should now have an understanding of versioning for the corresponding objects, as well as a high-level understanding of the Metadata Repository. In the next chapter, we'll look at how to optimize data access.

6 Data access optimizations

In this chapter, I will introduce the process for optimizing data access. We will learn how to use aggregates and how to measure an object's performance with statistics.

6.1 About BW system performance

Any SAP BW project starts with a business requirement that has to be analyzed. During this initial phase, it is very important to involve different types of users (from the business, from BW administration, from the data warehouse team, etc.). This phase ensures that the necessary resources are dedicated to the project. After the SAP BW deployment, the system will need regular maintenance in order to optimize performance. Often, the performance is related to the query execution time. One technique for improving performance is to use aggregates.

6.2 Using aggregates

An *aggregate* is an object that contains a smaller dataset of the InfoCube on which the aggregate is defined. This definition is created using specific criteria (such as a characteristic InfoObject). When an aggregate has been defined, the aggregated dataset can be read directly from the aggregated object.

> **BW objects and aggregates**
>
> SAP BW aggregates can only be defined in standard or real-time InfoCubes.

The load on the system is then relieved through the performance of summarization during the query execution.

Benefits

Using aggregates is beneficial because they:

- ► Improve query execution
- ► Reduce the volume of data that has to be read from the database
- ► Reduce the database workload during query runtime

Example scenario

You load data daily because you have to create calculations for a weekly report. Without aggregates, those calculations will run during query execution. Large datasets and complex calculations will dramatically slow down the query runtime. In this scenario, is useful to pre-calculate the required data and store it in a smaller InfoCube. The query runs against the smaller dataset and performance is better. This process is realized using aggregates.

> **Aggregates and rollup**
>
> When data is loaded into an InfoCube, the corresponding aggregates must also be loaded. This is called the rollup process (see *Rollup aggregates* on page 106). If you fail to perform a rollup, the data will not be available for reporting purposes.

Aggregates analysis

To use aggregates effectively, you have to consider the queries that are defined for the InfoCube. In fact, aggregates have to be useful from the queries' point of view. In other words, does the aggregate improve query performance? Does it solve a specific performance issue? Is it being used?

Aggregates optimization

The tools provided by SAP BW for analyzing aggregates are the query monitor and BW statistics (see Section 6.3). These tools can make suggestions on how to improve query performance or they can propose new aggregates.

6.2.1 Defining the aggregates

Aggregates are created by selecting specific criteria to make sure the aggregate's objects are smaller than the InfoCube on which they are defined. The selections can be made based on:

- ▶ Characteristics
- ▶ Navigational attributes
- ▶ Hierarchies

There is also other information that is useful for defining an aggregate. Let us take a closer look at the factors that should be considered when defining an aggregate.

Compounded characteristics

Compounded characteristics are always included in the aggregate definition (see *Compounding tab* on page 36).

Dependent characteristics

All characteristics that are derived from the one included in the aggregate should be also included in the aggregate definition.

Restrictions on multiple characteristics

Restricting multiple characteristics to a fixed value or hierarchy makes the system use the AND statement during the SQL creation.

Time-dependent aggregates

When the aggregate includes a time-dependent attribute, the entire aggregate has to be made time-dependent.

> **Using time-dependent aggregates**
>
> This aggregation should be avoided whenever possible because it is a resource-consuming process.

Exception aggregation

When a key figure is used in the aggregate it is defined as an exception aggregation (see *Aggregation tab* on page 40). In this case, the characteristic part of the exception must be included in the aggregate as well.

6.2.2 Creating an aggregate

To create an aggregate, go to the MODELING section of the DWW and right-click the InfoCube you want to aggregate. Select MAINTAIN AGGREGATES. On the next screen, you can choose to perform the aggregation yourself or ask the system to propose the aggregate. In our scenario, we will create the aggregate ourselves. The screen shown in Figure 6.1 appears. The left-hand panel shows the InfoCube objects and the middle panel shows the working space.

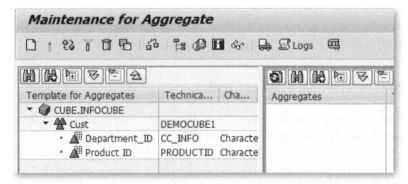

Figure 6.1: Aggregates initial screen

To add an aggregate, simply drag and drop the object selected from the left-hand panel to the working area. Now you have to enter the aggregate description. Once you have done this, the screen shown in Figure 6.2 appears. In our scenario, we aggregate using the Department ID, which represents the identification of a department within a company. This InfoCube reports the sales volume for each department.

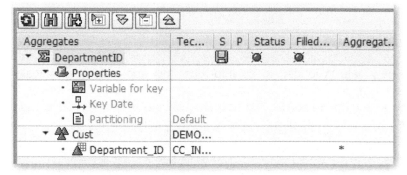

Figure 6.2: Aggregates working area

By right-clicking the DEPARTMENT_ID object, you can decide whether the aggregation should consider all of the values for the InfoCube (option ALL CHARACTERISTIC VALUES) or a specific value (option FIXED VALUE). If the object has a hierarchy, you can choose it from the HIERARCHY LEVEL option.

After completing this definition, press the ACTIVATION button ( ) to fill in the aggregate. On the next screen, press the START button to begin the activation. You can now see that the STATUS and the FILLED columns of the aggregate have turned green (see Figure 6.3), which indicates a successful activation and filling of the aggregate. You can view the loaded data by pressing the AGGREGATE DATA button ( ).

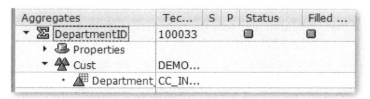

Figure 6.3: Activated aggregate

> **Queries and aggregates**
>
> When running a query, the BW system decides automatically which aggregates to use for a query to be more efficient. Thus, the query is defined on the InfoCube and not on the aggregate.

105

It is possible to create different aggregates on the same characteristic. This makes sense with different aggregation levels (aggregating on a FIXED VALUE or on a HIERARCHY).

Rollup aggregates

When new data is loaded to an InfoCube, this does not automatically update the aggregated data. This operation is referred to as a rollup. It can be executed manually from the ROLLUP tab in the InfoCube (see Figure 6.4), or it can be part of a process chain automation.

Figure 6.4: InfoCube Rollup tab

Rollup and queries

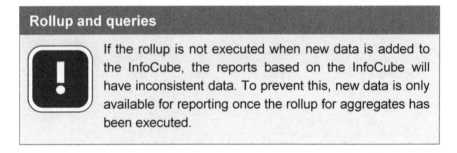

If the rollup is not executed when new data is added to the InfoCube, the reports based on the InfoCube will have inconsistent data. To prevent this, new data is only available for reporting once the rollup for aggregates has been executed.

Compressing aggregates

Aggregates have two fact tables and like InfoCubes, can be compressed (see Figure 4.7). You can execute compression from the ROLLUP tab of the InfoCube (see Figure 6.4). Compression will take place because the checkbox COMPRESS AFTER ROLLUP in the AGGREGATES section of the tab is selected by default.

> **Compressing aggregates**
>
> I recommend compressing the InfoCube first and then its aggregates.

Process chains and aggregates

Aggregates can be automated into a process chain by following these basic steps:

1. Start the process.
2. Delete InfoCube indexes.
3. Execute the InfoPackage.
4. Run the DTP.
5. Create the InfoCube indexes.
6. Create the database statistics.
7. Rollup data into the aggregates.

Change run and aggregates

When new data is loaded to the InfoCube, it may contain modifications to the master data attributes of an object. To apply those modifications to the aggregates, you have to execute a change run. You can do this manually from the TOOLS menu by selecting APPLY HIERARCHY/ATTRIBUTE CHANGE (see Figure 6.5). On the next screen, click the INFOOBJECT LIST button. The list of characteristics for which a change run is required now appears.

Figure 6.5: Tools menu for the change run

> **Activating master data**
>
> Activating new master data does not automatically update the data aggregates. A change run will execute the update. The new data is not available for reporting until the change run has been executed.

6.3 BW statistics

The BW statistics tools record runtime for processes and events to prevent and solve performance issues. You will regularly need to verify the performances of InfoCubes, queries, aggregates, and all other objects that make use of the BW system. There are different ways of dealing with the performance of BW objects. You can define settings for individual objects (see Section 6.3.1), you can use the technical BI Content (see Section 6.3.2), or you can execute the BW Administration Cockpit (see Section 6.3.3).

6.3.1 Settings for BW statistics

Using the menu TOOLS • SETTINGS FOR BW STATISTICS (see Figure 6.6) of the DWW allows you to check whether BW objects are configured to record statistical data. BW objects are classified into four categories: QUERY, INFOPROVIDER, WEB TEMPLATE, and WORKBOOK (see Figure 6.7).

Goto	Tools	Environment	Settings	System	Help
	Apply Hierarchy/Attribute Change...				Ctrl+F9
	Maintain Hierarchy Versions				Ctrl+Shift+F9
	Settings for BW Statistics				Ctrl+Shift+F10
	Extraction Monitor				Shift+Ctrl+0

Figure 6.6: Settings for BW statistics

On each tab, you can search for and select the object statistics that should be recorded in the BW system.

Figure 6.7: Statistics objects categories

6.3.2 Technical BI Content

The technical BI Content can be accessed from the DWW, under the InfoArea BUSINESS INFORMATION WAREHOUSE, BI STATISTICS. It provides statistical information on the use and performance of all of the other SAP BW objects. These objects also build the foundation of the BW Administration Cockpit (see Section 6.3.3).

6.3.3 BW Administration Cockpit

You can use the BW Administration Cockpit to monitor and manage the performance of a BW system using either SAP NetWeaver Portal or the BusinessObjects Dashboard. The following preconfigured dashboards are available:

- 0XCLS_0TCT_BW_MONITOR
- 0XCLS_0TCT_PC_DETAILS
- 0XCLS_0TCT_REPORTING_DETAIL

The BW Administration Cockpit is used to:

- Track the status of BW objects, BW operations, etc.
- Optimize the performance of BW activities
- Manage multiple BW systems from a central location

Figure 6.8 illustrates the architecture of the BW Administration Cockpit. The interaction between BW statistics, technical BI Content, and the BW Administration Cockpit is based on this architecture.

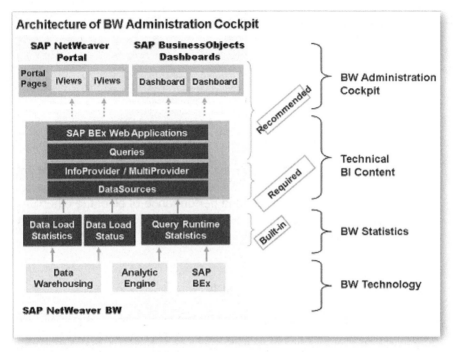

Figure 6.8: BW Administration Cockpit (source: help.sap.com)

To use the BW Administration Cockpit, you must have the proper administration rights on the BW system and you have to activate the technical BI Content. This process goes beyond the purpose of this book, but you can find additional information in this article from the SAP Help Portal (see http://help.sap.com/saphelp_nw73/helpdata/en/4e/1c145b0bf01a24e10000000a42189e/content.htm).

6.3.4 Query Monitor

The Query Monitor is another tool available in SAP BW that provides statistics on query performance. It is available via transaction code RSRT and is shown in Figure 6.9. Simply search for a query and then press one of the available buttons to obtain statistical information about the selected query.

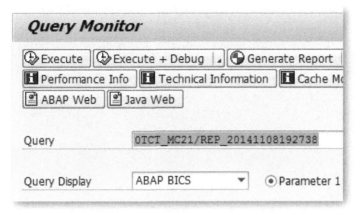

Figure 6.9: Query Monitor (SAP BW screenshot)

6.4 Summary

In this chapter, you learned how to use one of the fundamentals of system optimization—aggregates. This includes using ROLLUP, COMPRESSION, and CHANGE RUN functions. Furthermore, I introduced BW statistics as another way to improve the BW system. Next, we will learn how to design queries.

7 Designing queries

In this chapter you will get to know one of the SAP BEx tools: the BEx Query Designer. It is used to create queries using the data available from the different InfoProviders.

7.1 Business Explorer (BEx) tools

The BEx tools are a set of components that helps with the process of transforming data into useful information with the final result shown in a report. This process is realized by creating a query that interrogates the data source (InfoProviders). The different BEx tools are shown in the Figure 7.1.

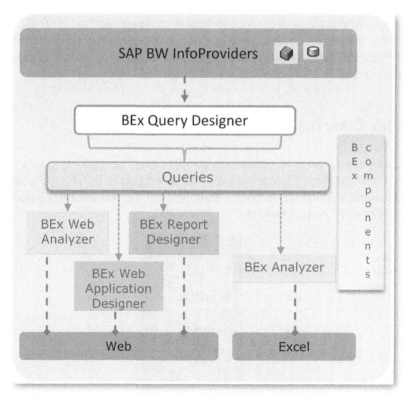

Figure 7.1: SAP BEx components

BEx Query Designer is the tool used to created queries on InfoProviders. These queries are available for reporting and analysis for the following BEx tools:

- **BEx Web Analyzer** is a web-based application that can read queries or even directly access InfoProviders for ad hoc analysis.
- **BEx Web Application Designer** is used to create applications with components called web items such as filters, buttons, charts, tables, etc. These applications are saved as a web template and made available on a web portal.
- **BEx Report Designer** is the tool used to generate formatted reports. It was removed from BW after the 7.0 release.
- **BEx Analyzer** is used for creating reports and analysis based on Microsoft Excel. An SAP add-in allows connection to InfoProviders directly from Excel. The application created is saved as a workbook.

All of these applications are installed locally together with the SAP GUI logon (see Section 1.2.3) and they are accessible from the program list of a Windows system following the path START MENU • PROGRAMS • BUSINESS EXPLORER.

7.2 BEx Query Designer overview

BEx Query Designer is the stand-alone application for building queries for BW InfoProviders. You can run it, without logging in to SAP BW, directly from the Windows start menu (see Figure 7.2). You will be prompted for the user ID and password.

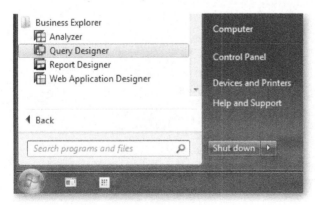

Figure 7.2: Start BEx Query Designer

7.2.1 BEx Query Designer intial screen

Once you have logged in to BEx Query Designer, the default screen as shown in Figure 7.3 appears. There are several working areas: the INFOPROVIDER, the FILTER, the PROPERTIES, the MESSAGES, and the ROWS/COLUMNS areas.

Figure 7.3: BEx Query Designer default screen

InfoProvider area

To begin designing a query, you first have to select an InfoProvider. This area displays the SAP BW objects that are present in the InfoProvider selected for building the query. Choose a new InfoProvider by pressing the NEW button (🗋) or by selecting NEW from the QUERY menu (see Figure 7.4).

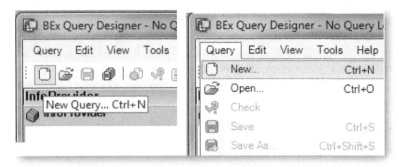

Figure 7.4: New InfoProvider

If you want to open an existing query instead, click the OPEN button () or select OPEN from the QUERY menu. Either way, the key figures and the dimensions of the selected InfoProvider appear under this area once you have selected it.

> **InfoProvider and queries**
>
> Remember that a query can be related to only one InfoProvider. In order to use data from different InfoProviders, you have to define MultiProviders or InfoSets.

Filter area

The filter area is composed of two distinct sections: the CHARACTERISTIC RESTRICTIONS and the DEFAULT VALUES. They are both used to declare query filters but they work in different ways and provide different results. The CHARACTERISTIC RESTRICTIONS, also referred to as global filters, apply to the entire query result and cannot be modified after the query execution. The DEFAULT VALUES are local filters, i.e., their values can be entered initially and can be modified after the query execution.

Properties area

In this area, you maintain the properties of the selected object of the query. Based on your selection, multiple tabs can appear. If you do not choose anything, the query properties are displayed.

Message area

Errors, warnings, and messages related to the query are shown in this area.

Rows/Columns area

You access this area by pressing the corresponding tab (Rows/Columns). Here, you define the layout of the future report by dragging and dropping the objects required (see Figure 7.5). The FREE CHARACTERISTICS area is for objects that you do not want to include in the initial query but that you want to make available to users for drilldown. The PREVIEW section shows a preview of the report layout.

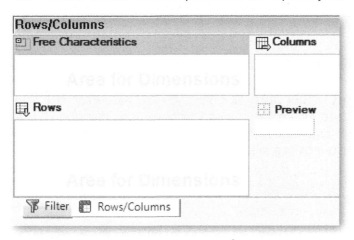

Figure 7.5: Rows/Columns area

7.2.2 BEx Query Designer toolbar

The QUERY DESIGNER screen contains a toolbar that is context-specific, i.e., buttons are activated depending on the actions you are performing on the query. Some functions are quite obvious, such as NEW, OPEN, and SAVE. We will focus on only a few, namely the CELLS, the CONDITIONS, and the EXCEPTIONS button (see Figure 7.6).

Figure 7.6: Query design toolbar (SAP screenshot)

☞ The CELLS icon is only active when a structure is identified in the ROWS/COLUMNS area (later on I will explain how a structure works). Clicking on the CELLS icon opens the CELLS tab where you can create formulas and selection conditions for individual cells. This is useful when a cell appears at the intersection of two structures.

▦ Pressing the CONDITIONS icon makes the CONDITIONS tab appear. In this area, you can define the parameters for each key figure identified in the query. For example, you show only the quantities that are greater than a certain value.

▦ Clicking on the EXCEPTIONS icon makes the EXCEPTIONS tab appear. In this area, you can set up alerts based on certain key figure value levels. The alerts appear in different colors in a report.

7.3 Creating a query

To create a query in BEx Query Designer, you first have to choose your INFOPROVIDER (see Figure 7.4). Once you have done that, the objects (key figures and dimensions) that are part of the InfoProvider definition appear in the INFOPROVIDER area (see Figure 7.7).

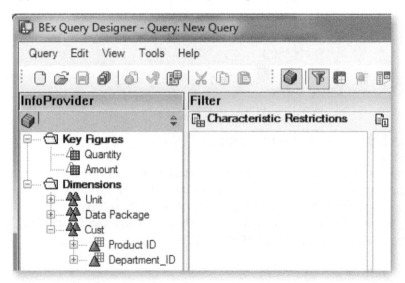

Figure 7.7: InfoProvider objects

You can now begin to define your query. Start by selecting filters or by selecting the rows and columns.

7.3.1 Selecting filters

From the FILTER tab, we can restrict the result to the values that are needed from the query definition. For our scenario, we want to know the number of products sold (quantity) by department 1200. Drag and drop the dimension DEPARTMENT_ID from the INFOPROVIDER area to the CHARACTERISTICS RESTRICTIONS area. Double-click the object to open the selection screen (see Figure 7.8). From the SHOW field, there are several ways of searching for the value required. If you use the SINGLE VALUES option, all of the related values are shown. Double-click the value 1200 to make it appear in the CHOSEN SELECTIONS area. You can also decide (if required) to exclude the value from the result. To do that, highlight the value and press the EXCLUDE FROM SELECTION button (see Figure 7.9).

Confirm your selection by pressing the OK button. The CHARACTERISTICS RESTRICTIONS area now shows your selection (see Figure 7.10).

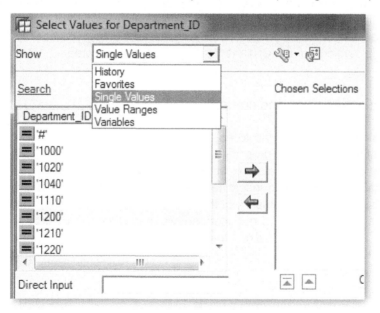

Figure 7.8: Filter selection

DESIGNING QUERIES

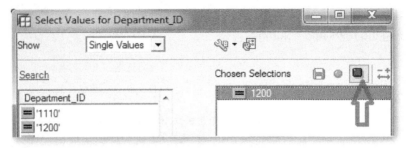

Figure 7.9: Exclude selection button

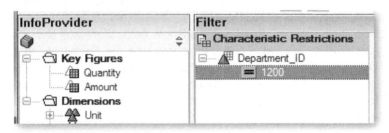

Figure 7.10: Restriction selected

As already described, the CHARACTERISTIC RESTRICTIONS (also referred to as global filters) apply the selection to the entire query result and cannot be modified after the query has been executed. Obviously, you can append multiple objects to the CHARACTERISTIC RESTRICTIONS area.

7.3.2 Selecting rows and columns

Select the ROWS/COLUMNS tab to enter the area where the query layout can be defined. Drag and drop the objects you want to appear in the report into the rows and columns areas. A layout preview is displayed automatically each time you insert new objects. Generally, the rows are used to display the characteristics of the future report and key figures are used in the columns area. For our scenario, we drag DEPARTMENT_ID into the ROWS area and the QUANTITY into the COLUMNS area, as shown in Figure 7.11.

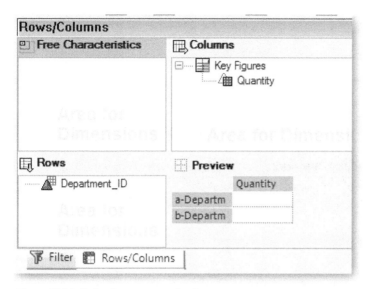

Figure 7.11: Selecting rows and columns

You can now verify the correctness of the query you have designed by pressing . The MESSAGE area informs you whether the query is correct. If it is, then the query is ready to be saved to the SAP system. The saved query will be available in the FAVORITES folder in SAP BW. Executing the query ( ) from the BEx Query Designer opens the BEx Web Analyzer with your default browser.

7.3.3 Selecting conditions

The condition parameters restrict the data records in order to allow only the most important information to be displayed. Pressing the CONDITIONS button ( ) opens the CONDITIONS tab where you can start to declare a new condition by right-clicking the condition area. This creates the structure of an empty object named CONDITION 1 by the system. Double-click this object to start editing the condition (see Figure 7.12). You can modify the condition name in the DESCRIPTION field.

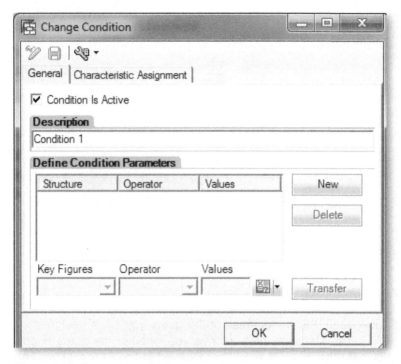

Figure 7.12: Change Condition screen

To define condition parameters, click the NEW button. This activates the fields KEY FIGURES, OPERATOR, and VALUES (see Figure 7.13). The key figures list will contain the objects defined in our query as key figures, which is QUANTITY in our case.

Figure 7.13: Condition fields activated (SAP screenshot)

Now select one OPERATOR from the list (see Figure 7.14) and a value. Here you can enter a manual number or you can create your own variable (we will cover creating variables later in this chapter).

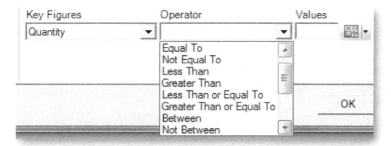

Figure 7.14: Selecting the operator

Once you have finished, press the TRANSFER button (see Figure 7.15) and the selections then appear in the conditions list. The query result is filtered according to these parameters, i.e., it shows only the quantities that have a value greater than 500. Click OK to confirm your selections. The condition is now saved in the query definition.

Figure 7.15: Conditions selected

Key figure properties

Executing the query as it is will have the following result:

Table	
Department_ID	Quantity
1020	620 KG
1040	560 KG
Overall Result	**1.975 KG**

Figure 7.16: Query result in BEx Analyzer

It correctly displays the departments with more than 500 kg sold but it gives the wrong total. In fact, the sum should be 1180 kg and not 1975 kg. To resolve this inconsistency, we need to go back to our query definition. In particular, to the properties of our QUANTITY object declared in the COLUMNS area. Double-click the object to display the QUANTITY properties (see Figure 7.17).

123

DESIGNING QUERIES

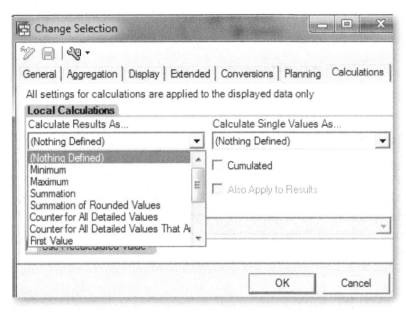

Figure 7.17: Editing the key figure quantity

Go to the CALCULATIONS tab. From the field CALCULATE RESULTS AS..., select SUMMATION. This setting will correct the query result.

7.3.4 Selecting exceptions

The exceptions settings will provide a different display of cells. In fact, selecting the exceptions highlights the cells that fall under the exception definition. Clicking the EXCEPTIONS button ( ) opens the corresponding area. This creates the structure of an empty object named EXCEPTIONS 1 by the system. Double-click the object to start editing the exception (see Figure 7.18). You can modify the exception name in the DESCRIPTION field. Similarly to the condition screen (see Figure 7.12), you define exception parameters by clicking the NEW button. This activates the fields ALERT LEVEL, OPERATOR, and VALUES (see Figure 7.19). Each selection in the ALERT LEVEL list corresponds to a color alert. GOOD1 displays a green cell and BAD1 a red cell. In our scenario, we want to indicate the quantity cell values that are greater than 600 (see Figure 7.20). Click the TRANSFER button to confirm those selections. Before completing the exception editing, we have to tell the system which query element those exceptions must apply to. To do so, go to the DEFINITION tab (see Figure 7.21).

Designing Queries

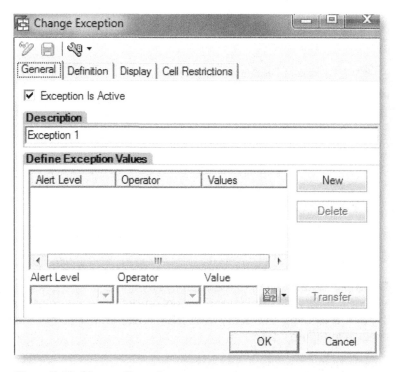

Figure 7.18: Change Exception screen

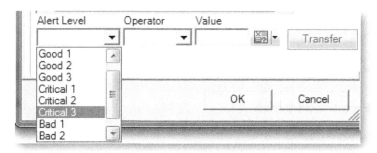

Figure 7.19: Exceptions fields activated

Figure 7.20: Exceptions selected

125

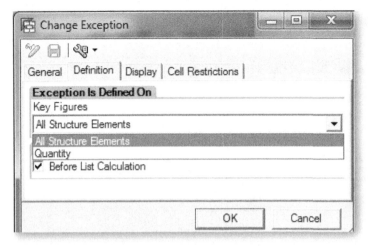

Figure 7.21: Exception definition tab

We want to apply the exception to the quantity key figure, so we select it from the KEY FIGURES list. Confirm the exception definition by pressing the OK button. Executing the query with BEx Analyzer will output the result as shown in Figure 7.22.

Table Department_ID	Quantity
1020	620 KG
1040	560 KG
Overall Result	**1.180 KG**

Figure 7.22: Exception query result

7.3.5 Creating structures

Structures define the basic layout of the query for a row or column. There are two types of structures based on the object they contain:

- ▶ Key figure structures
- ▶ Characteristic structures

>
> **Structure figures**
>
> A maximum of two structures are allowed in the query definition. Only one can contain key figures. Using structures is not mandatory. Structures can be reused in other queries.

Structures are identified by the structure icon (▦).

Key figure structures

As you have probably noticed, the BEx Query Designer automatically creates a key figure structure when you include a key figure in the query definition (see Figure 7.11). Since only one type of this structure can be declared in a query, if you want to add another key figure, it must be included in the same structure, as shown in Figure 7.23.

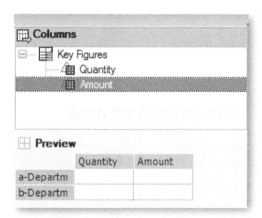

Figure 7.23: Key figure structure

Selections and formulas can be included in the key figure structure definition.

>
> **Key figure components**
>
> A characteristic, or a selection without a key figure, cannot be included in the key figure structure.

DESIGNING QUERIES

An example of a characteristic used with a key figure structure is when you want to restrict the key figure to a specific characteristic and make it appear in the report layout, as shown in Figure 7.24. The report shows yearly quantities sold per department. A query definition requires the following changes to achieve this result.

Table		
Department_ID	Quantity2013	Quantity 2014
1000	150 KG	
1020	160 KG	140 KG
2000	245 KG	580 KG
Overall Result	555 KG	720 KG

Figure 7.24: Report result

First, the characteristic CALENDAR YEAR (0CALYEAR) must be part of the InfoCube definition (this is done in SAP BW). This will make it visible in the INFOPROVIDER area of the BEx Query Designer (see Figure 7.25).

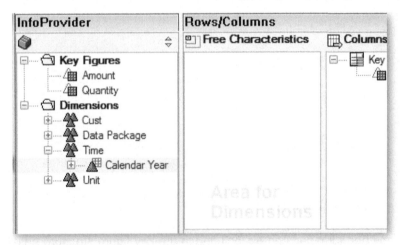

Figure 7.25: Calendar year characteristic

Next, right-click the QUANTITY key figure structure to edit it (see Figure 7.26). The CHANGE SELECTION screen opens (see Figure 7.27).

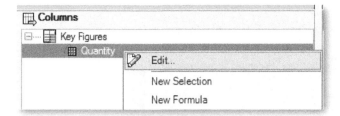

Figure 7.26: Editing the key figures structure

Drag and drop the characteristic CALENDAR YEAR from the INFOPROVIDER list to the DETAILS OF THE SELECTION area. Double-clicking it opens the list of values available for the calendar year. From this list, choose 2013 to complete our example. Confirm by pressing the OK button. Change the description to QUANTITY 2013. You should now have the settings as shown in Figure 7.28.

Now create the QUANTITY 2014 characteristic. Begin by right-clicking the KEY FIGURE structure, then select NEW SELECTION and perform the same steps as for QUANTITY 2013.

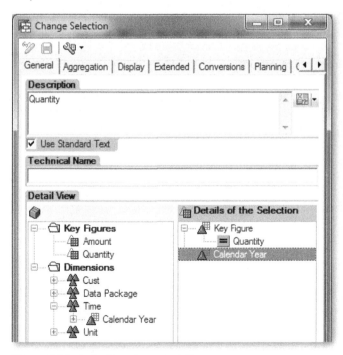

Figure 7.27: Selecting characteristics

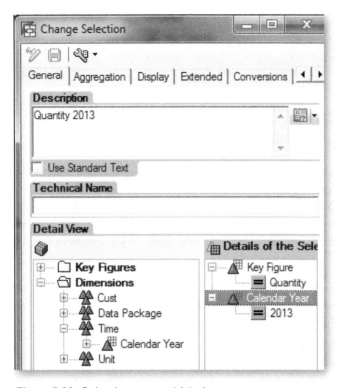

Figure 7.28: Calendar year restricted

The resulting query definition should look like the one shown in Figure 7.29.

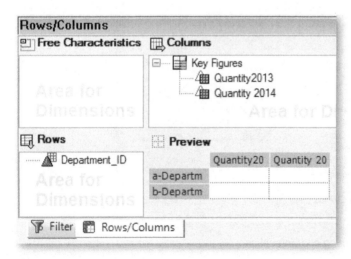

Figure 7.29: Query definition with structure

Executing the query with BEx Analyzer will give you the following result (see Figure 7.30):

Table		
Department_ID	Quantity2013	Quantity 2014
1000	150 KG	
1020	160 KG	140 KG
2000	245 KG	580 KG
Overall Result	555 KG	720 KG

Figure 7.30: Query result

What if you now also need to show the difference in percentage between those two years? The answer is to create a formula.

Creating a formula

We want to add a column that shows the percentage difference between years. Right-click the KEY FIGURE structure and select NEW FORMULA (see Figure 7.26). Double-click the new formula object to edit it. This opens the CHANGE FORMULA screen (see Figure 7.31). Begin by changing the DESCRIPTION to % DIFF. Next, define the logic of the formula as follows:

((Quantity 2014 - Quantity2013)/(Quantity2013))*100

We also need to define how we handle the zero values as a result of division using the NDIV0 function, which is available from the OPERATORS area in the folder DATA FUNCTIONS.

Create the formula by double-clicking each component to bring it into the DETAIL VIEW as it appears below.

Executing the new query definition displays the column %DIFF. with the corresponding percentage difference between those two years, as indicated in the formula in Figure 7.32.

Figure 7.31: Changing a formula

```
Detail View
NDIV0 ( ( 'Quantity 2014' - 'Quantity2013' ) /
('Quantity2013' ) ) * 100
```

Figure 7.32: Formula detail

Characteristic structure

You use a characteristic structure when you want to show a distinct number of characteristic values in a particular sequence. To create a new structure, right-click the ROWS/COLUMNS area and then choose NEW STRUCTURE.

This creates the structure object in the chosen area. The STRUCTURE still needs to be defined. Right-click the structure (see Figure 7.33) to select a structure component (NEW SELECTION or NEW FORMULA).

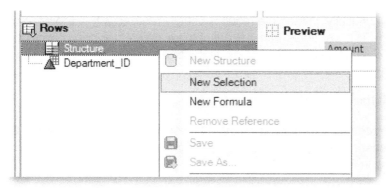

Figure 7.33: Selecting structure components

Choosing NEW SELECTION opens the window shown in Figure 7.34, where you can define the characteristic settings. The dimension that you select for the structure can be also restricted to a specific value.

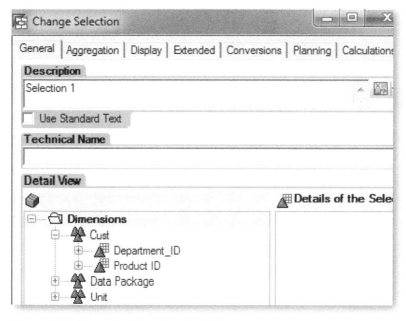

Figure 7.34: New selection characteristic

7.3.6 Creating variables

In a query definition, variables are used to allow users to dynamically change the result of data before the query is executed. Creating a variable to dynamically change the result is usually realized with a prompt or a selection. The variables can be defined for different types of objects, such as characteristics, hierarchies, texts, or formulas.

Characteristic variable

For our scenario, we create a variable based on the DEPARTMENT_ID characteristic. This variable can be created from the INFOPROVIDER area as shown in Figure 7.35.

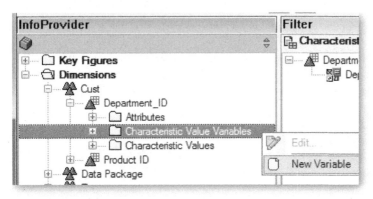

Figure 7.35: Characteristic new variable

This step creates a NEW VARIABLE object. Double-click it to open the CHANGE VARIABLE screen (see Figure 7.36).

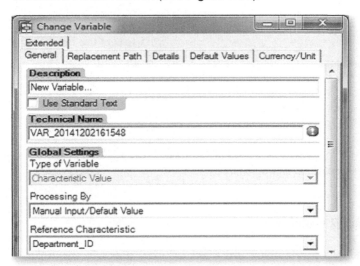

Figure 7.36: Editor for changing variables

Next, modify the DESCRIPTION and the TECHNICAL NAME. On the DETAILS tab, you can define whether the variable is mandatory or optional and make it available when the query is executed by selecting the checkbox VARIABLE IS READY FOR INPUT (see Figure 7.37).

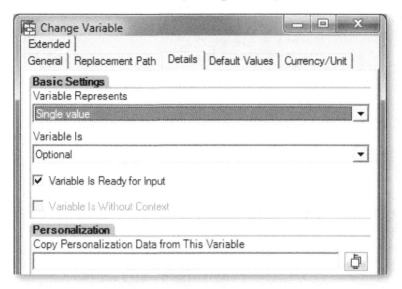

Figure 7.37: Details tab for variables

Variable is

 If the variable has been declared as OPTIONAL and the user leaves it blank during query execution, the query runs for all the values of the characteristic to which the variable refers.

Finally, the DEFAULT VALUES tab allows you to select the default value for which the query will run. Confirm your settings. The new variable is now displayed in the folder CHARACTERISTIC VALUE VARIABLES of the DEPARTMENT_ID characteristic (see Figure 7.38) and can be used as a characteristic restriction.

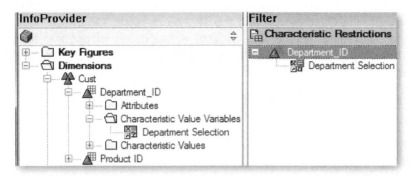

Figure 7.38: Characteristic variable created

7.4 Summary

In this chapter, you learned how to use the BEx Query Designer to build a query for analysis. In the next chapter, you will learn how to leverage the BEx Analyzer for reporting activities.

8 Reporting

A report shows the formatted result for a query. In this chapter, I will explain how to use an SAP reporting tool called the BEx Analyzer.

8.1 SAP reporting tools

Within the BEx suite (see Section 7.1), SAP provides two tools for reporting purposes:

- BEx Web Analyzer
- BEx Analyzer

The first one is web-based, while the second one works with Microsoft Excel and is the main topic in this chapter.

8.2 BEx Analyzer

BEX Analyzer is installed locally along with the SAP GUI logon (see Section 1.2.3) and is accessible from the program list of a Windows system following the path START MENU • PROGRAMS• BUSINESS EXPLORER (see Figure 7.2). An Excel session opens when you run BEx Analyzer. The corresponding functionalities are available on the ADD-INS tab (see Figure 8.1).

Figure 8.1: BEx Analyzer Add-Ins tab

8.2.1 Running the report

To have access to the report results, you first have to establish a connection to the SAP system. You can do so by clicking the CONNECTION button (%) or by selecting the OPEN QUERY folder (📂). After logging in, you have to select an existing query from the BW system. The report will be based on this selection. The query runs immediately after the selection and the result is displayed in an Excel sheet. If the query contains a variable definition (see *Characteristic variable* on page 134), a prompt screen appears before the query is executed, asking you to select the variable value (see Figure 8.2). After you have completed this selection, the result is shown in an Excel sheet.

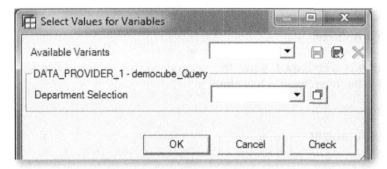

Figure 8.2: Selecting the value for a variable

Together with the result, the Excel sheet contains three buttons: CHART, FILTER, and INFORMATION (see Figure 8.3).

Department_ID	Quantity2013	Quantity 2014	% Diff.
1000	150 KG		-100,00
1020	160 KG	140 KG	-12,50
2000	245 KG	580 KG	136,73
Overall Result	555 KG	720 KG	29,73

Figure 8.3: Report result

The CHART button converts the result into a chart that you can edit like a standard Excel chart. The FILTER button displays the elements defined as filters in the query.

Figure 8.4: Filter selection

The INFORMATION button provides technical details about the query that has been executed. This result can be saved in what SAP calls a *workbook*.

8.2.2 Playing with the report

Next, we will cover two ways of handling the report results: filters and navigation.

Filters

Clicking on the FILTER button displays the elements defined as filters in the query (see Figure 8.4). Using the filters restricts the query result. You select a filter value by double-clicking the corresponding cell or by entering the value directly in the cell.

Navigation

There are additional options available from the FILTER area. You can access them by right-clicking a filter cell (see Figure 8.5).

Reporting

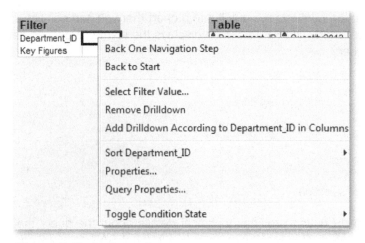

Figure 8.5: Navigation options

The BACK ONE NAVIGATION STEP option undoes your last change in the workbook. The BACK TO START option brings the report back to the initial state when the query was first executed. For SELECT FILTER VALUE, see *Filters* on page 139). The DRILLDOWN options allow you to add or remove (in columns or rows) selected characteristics. The same operation is possible by dragging and dropping both from the FILTER area and from the TABLE area. The result is refreshed according to your drilldown options. The SORT DEPARTMENT_ID option sorts the result by Department ID. If the characteristic has attributes, you can select them from the PROPERTIES screen. From the QUERY PROPERTIES dialog, you can view some query information and can change some settings for the data layout. The TOGGLE CONDITION STATE option allows you to enable or disable the condition declared in the query (if any).

A context menu is also available by right-clicking the table elements. You can swap the axes of the analysis or, swap one element with another.

8.2.3 Creating the report

The BEx Analyzer has functionality to help you modify the report layout and to perform some analyses: the DESIGN toolbar and the ANALYSIS toolbar (see Figure 8.6). Let us take a closer look at the DESIGN toolbar next.

REPORTING

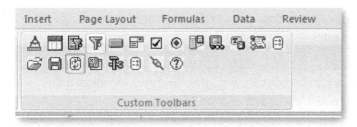

Figure 8.6: BEx Analyzer toolbars

The design toolbar

Using functionality in the design toolbar, you can build your own analysis application within Excel.

△ This button allows you to switch to the design mode or back to the report result.

▦ Clicking this button inserts the *analysis grid* into the design mode. The initial query result is displayed in the analysis grid, making this object an important component for the workbook.

▧ Clicking this button inserts the *navigation pane* into the design mode. This component displays all elements that can be used to navigate through the data. The initial filters of the query are part of a navigation pane.

▼ Clicking this button inserts the *filter* item into the design mode and displays all the filters applied to the query.

▭ This icon inserts a button into the application. You can then configure the behavior of this button when it is clicked.

▭ ☑ ⊙ These buttons respectively insert a dropdown box, a checkbox, and a radio button into the application design. They are used to provide users with more options for displaying data.

▦ Clicking this button inserts the *conditions* item into the design mode and displays all the conditions applied to the query. The user can set the condition as active or inactive.

141

🖳 This button lists the exceptions used in the query; it works similarly to the conditions.

🖹 This item inserts text information into the design. A list of different text elements can be chosen, e.g., display query technical name, display last refreshed, or last changed by, etc.

📜 The message that may be generated during navigation or analysis (warnings, errors) can be displayed in the report using this item.

⊟ This button opens the WORKBOOK SETTINGS screen, where you can define some workbook properties.

The analysis toolbar

The analysis toolbar presents the options shown in Figure 8.7.

Figure 8.7: Analysis toolbar

We have already seen the OPEN FOLDER 📂 and the CONNECTION buttons. Now let us take a look at the remaining buttons.

🔄 This button refreshes the query result.

📋 For the queries that contain variables, clicking this icon opens the variable selection screen.

🧩 This button provides access to the BEx applications.

⊟ The global settings button allows you to maintain various parameters in the BEx Analyzer (see Figure 8.8).

❓ This button displays SAP help documentation.

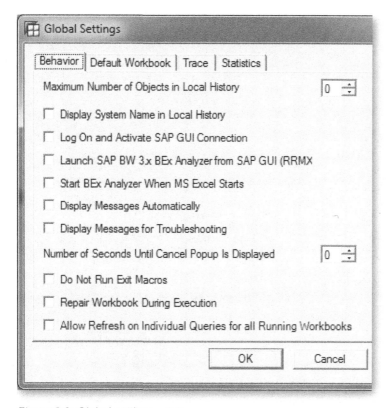

Figure 8.8: Global settings window

Creating an analysis application

Now that we understand BEx functionality, we can build a simple analysis application. Our scenario will be to create a dropdown box for selecting the Department ID and an option for filtering the result using a condition.

Log in to the BEx Analyzer and create a new document using the NEW icon ( ). Select a few cells in the middle of the document and click the INSERT ANALYSIS GRID button ( ) to insert it in the workbook. Double-click the designed item to open the PROPERTIES dialog (see Figure 8.9) for the analysis grid. You must select a DATAPROVIDER, i.e., a query from which to retrieve the data. Confirm your selection by pressing the OK button. This will bring you back to the workbook.

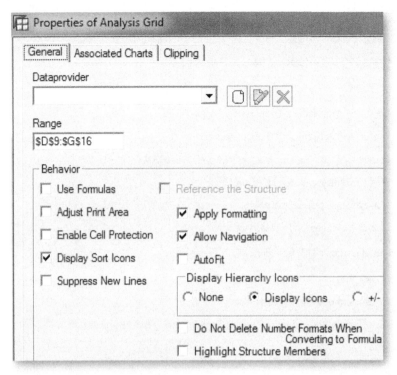

Figure 8.9: Properties of Analysis Grid

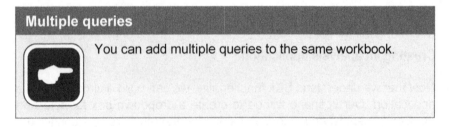

Next, select the cell where you want to insert the dropdown box and press the corresponding button ( ). Double-click the designed item to open the PROPERTIES OF THE DROPDOWN BOX screen (see Figure 8.10).

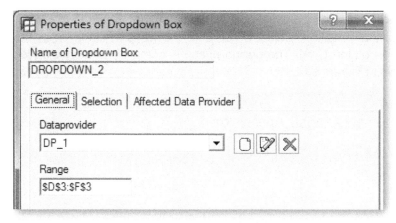

Figure 8.10: Dropdown box properties

Open the SELECTION tab to assign a query element (CHARACTERISTIC/STRUCTURE) to the dropdown box (see Figure 8.11). In our scenario it is the DEPARTMENT_ID.

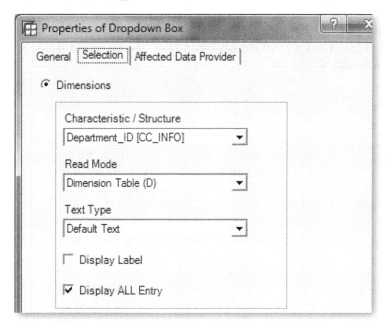

Figure 8.11: Selection tab

Click OK to return to the workbook. The last element to add to this application is the condition. Select a cell from the workbook and press the CONDITION button (🔳). The design phase is complete and should look as shown in Figure 8.12.

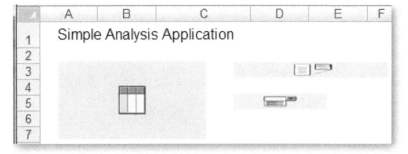

Figure 8.12: Analysis application design

Pressing the toggle button (🔺) displays the query result with the elements we have just designed, i.e., the analysis grid, the dropdown box, and the condition filter (see Figure 8.13). The first element shows the dataset, the second one allows you to select which department must be displayed in the dataset, and the condition filter can be set to active to influence the data result.

	A	B	C	D
1	Simple Analysis Application			
2				
3	Department_ID	Quantity2013	Quantity 2014	% Diff.
4	1000	150 KG		-100,00
5	1020	160 KG	140 KG	-12,50
6	2000	245 KG	580 KG	136,73
7	Overall Result	555 KG	720 KG	29,73
8				
9		QT2013>=160	Inactive	
10				
11				
12		All		
13		All		
14		#		
15		1000		
16		1020		
		1040		
		2000		

Figure 8.13: Workbook query result

You can now save and reuse the workbook.

8.3 Summary

This chapter guided you through the process of creating a report using BEx Analyzer. You now also have an understanding of how to use an existing query to build a report.

You have finished the book.

Sign up for our newsletter!

Learn more about new e-books?

Get exclusive free downloads.

Sign up for our newsletter!

Please visit us on *newsletter.espresso-tutorials.com* to find out more.

A About the Author

Gerardo di Giuseppe is a SAP business intelligence engineer with more than 14 years of experience in the IT industry. He has worked with multinational companies including Sony, P&G, and BNP Paribas along with public institutions such as the EU Parliament and Belgian Federal Police to establish their SAP BI strategy. He enjoys sharing his business intelligence knowledge and delivers training. Mr. di Giuseppe has a bachelor's degree in Management of Information Systems and a Master's in Business Intelligence from the CNAM University of Lille (France). He speaks Italian, French, and English fluently and has a working knowledge of Dutch. His active role in the IT world led him to found coproweb.be, a web platform that improves the communication among apartment owners and sunthetic.eu, a startup creating sustainable energy for IT devices.

B Index

A

ABAP 53
Activation queue 24
Active data 24
Active version 92
Administration tool 69
Aggregation 23
Alert message 87
Analysis 10
Analysis application 143
Analysis grid 141
Analysis toolbar 142
Application component 50
Architecture layer 12
Attribute 22
Automate 82

B

BEx Analyzer 114
BEx Query Designer 113
BEx tool 113
BEx Web Analyzer 121
BEx-Business Explorer 12
BI content 89
Business content 12
Business decision 8
Business intelligence 7
Business package 91
Business requirement 21
Business role 90
BW Administration cockpit 109
BW statistic 102

C

Catalog 98
Cell icon 118

Central database 8
Change log 24, 80
Change run 70
Change run and aggregate 107
Characteristic 9
Characteristic InfoObject 32
Characteristic restriction 116
Characteristic structure 132
Characteristic variable 134
Collapse 74
Collection 93
Collection mode 94
Compounded characteristic 103
Compounding 36
Compressing aggregate 106
Compression 74
Condition 118

D

Data cube 9
Data extraction 84
data flow 12
Data target 19
Data Transfer Process 62
Data warehouse 7
Data warehouse workbench 16
Data Warehouse Workbench 28
Database workload 102
DataSource 47
DataStore Object (DSO) 19
DB index 74
DB statistic 74
Delete change log 80
Delivery version 91
Delta mode 63

Design toolbar 141
Dimension 9
Display mode 33
Drilldown 140

E

Editing mode 33
ERP (Enterprise Resource Planning) 8
ETL process 8
Exception 118
Exception aggregation 104
Execution time 101
Extract, transform and load 47
Extraction process 47

F

Fact table 10
Filter area 116
Formula 131
Free characteristic 117

G

Granularity 10
Grouping 93

H

Hierarchy 10

I

Incorrect data 81
InfoArea 30
InfoCube 19
InfoObject 19
InfoObjectCatalog 30
InfoPackage 13, 47
InfoProvider 12

J

Join operation 26

K

Key figure 10
Key figure catalog 39
Key figure structure 127

M

Master data 22
Metadata repository 98
Microsoft Excel 114
Modified version 92
Monitor the execution 86
Multi-dimensional modelling 41
MultiProvider 19

N

Navigation 139
New Selection 132
Non-cumulative value 41

O

Object merge 97
Online Analytical Processing (OLAP) 8
Online Transaction Processing (OLTP) 8
Operational system 8
Operator 122

P

Performance 21
Persistent Staging Area 47
Predefined structure 89
Process chain 69
Prompt 134

Q

Query 19
Query monitor 102

R

Recurring task 82
Relational schema 8
Relationship 98
Repartitioning 71
Reporting 12, 137
request SID 80
Rollup 74
Rollup aggregate 106
Routine 53
Row/Column area 117

S

SAP Business Warehouse 12
SAP BW 9
SAP Easy Access 15
SAP ERP 8
SAP GUI 13
SAP HANA 24
Semantically partitioned InfoCube 23
SID Table 38
Simulate installation 97
Source system 13, 49
Staging area 13
Star Schema 10
Structure 126
Swap 140
System performance 101

T

Technical BI content 109
Time characteristic 21
Time-dependent aggregate 103
Transformation 58

U

Union operation 25
Unit 21

V

Variable 122
Volume of data 102

W

Workbook 139

D Disclaimer

This publication contains references to the products of SAP SE.

SAP, R/3, SAP NetWeaver, Duet, PartnerEdge, ByDesign, SAP BusinessObjects Explorer, StreamWork, and other SAP products and services mentioned herein as well as their respective logos are trademarks or registered trademarks of SAP SE in Germany and other countries.

Business Objects and the Business Objects logo, BusinessObjects, Crystal Reports, Crystal Decisions, Web Intelligence, Xcelsius, and other Business Objects products and services mentioned herein as well as their respective logos are trademarks or registered trademarks of Business Objects Software Ltd. Business Objects is an SAP company.

Sybase and Adaptive Server, iAnywhere, Sybase 365, SQL Anywhere, and other Sybase products and services mentioned herein as well as their respective logos are trademarks or registered trademarks of Sybase, Inc. Sybase is an SAP company.

SAP SE is neither the author nor the publisher of this publication and is not responsible for its content. SAP Group shall not be liable for errors or omissions with respect to the materials. The only warranties for SAP Group products and services are those that are set forth in the express warranty statements accompanying such products and services, if any. Nothing herein should be construed as constituting an additional warranty.

More Espresso Tutorials Books

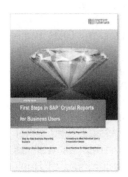

Anurag Barua:
First Steps in SAP® Crystal Reports
- ▶ Basic end-user navigation
- ▶ Creating a basic report from scratch
- ▶ Formatting to meet individual presentation needs

http://5017.espresso-tutorials.com/

Wolfgang Niefert
Business Intelligence with SAP® BI Edge
- ▶ Get to know the BI Edge Solutions 4.1
- ▶ Universe, Crystal Reports and Web Intelligence for beginners
- ▶ Learn about Connecting BI with SAP ERP (ECC 6.0)
- ▶ Case study with many screenshots and explanations

http://4040.espresso-tutorials.com

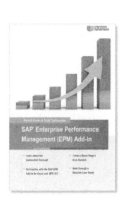

Kermit Bravo & Scott Cairncross:
SAP® Enterprise Performance Management (EPM) Add-In
- ▶ Learn about the Connection Concept
- ▶ Get familiar with the SAP EPM Add-In for Excel and BPC 10.1
- ▶ Create a Basic Report from Scratch
- ▶ Walk through a Detailed Case Study

http://5042.espresso-tutorials.com

Jörg Böke

SAP® BI Analysis Office — a Practical Guide

- ▶ Installation and prerequisites
- ▶ Analysis Excel Pivot, Ribbon and Context Menu Explained
- ▶ Enhanced reporting with API and Visual Basic (VBA)
- ▶ Comparison between Analysis Office AO and BEx

http://5096.espresso-tutorials.com

Shreekant Shiralkar & Deepak Sawant

SAP® BW Performance Optimization

- ▶ Use BW statistics effectively
- ▶ Leverage tools for extraction, loading, modeling and reporting
- ▶ Monitor performance using the Workload Monitor & database statistics
- ▶ Use indexes to understand key elements of performance

http://5102.espresso-tutorials.com

Rob Frye, Joe Darlak, Dr. Bjarne Berg

The SAP® BW to HANA Migration Handbook

- ▶ Proven Techniques for Planning and Executing a Successful Migration
- ▶ SAP BW on SAP HANA Sizing and Optimization
- ▶ Building a Solid Migration Business Case
- ▶ Step-by-Step Runbook for the Migration Process

http://5109.espresso-tutorials.com

Made in United States
North Haven, CT
24 June 2023